The
Antidote

How to Transform
Your Business for the
Extreme Challenges
of the 21st Century

Anand Sharma and Gary Hourselt

Managing Times Press
Durham, North Carolina

Published by Managing Times Press
4400 Ben Franklin Boulevard
Durham, NC 27704

Publisher's Cataloging-in-Publication Data
Sharma, Anand.

The antidote : how to transform your business for the extreme challenges of the 21st century. – Durham, NC : Managing Times Press, 2006.

p. ; cm.
ISBN: 0-9728099-4-5
ISBN13: 978-0-9728099-4-8

1. Industrial management-History-21st century. 2. Success in business-History-21st century. 3. Industrial organization-History-21st century. I. Hourselt, Gary. II. Title.

HD30.5 .S53 2006
658-dc22   2006922378

Book production and coordination by Jenkins Group, Inc. • www.bookpublishing.com
Interior design by Debbie Sidman
Cover design by Barbara Hodge

Printed in the United States of America
12 11 10 09 08 • 6 5 4 3 2

Dedication

This book is dedicated to the spouses and loved ones of all of the associates at TBM Consulting Group who provide their much needed support. Especially to Anu and Debbie, who help us remember to keep learning from the past, living in the moment, and working endlessly to make tomorrow even better than today.

Contents

Foreword

Amid the barrage of productivity and management books, it is particularly important to find one that captures the experiences and best practices that have propelled companies like Toyota, Pella, Dell, and others to market leadership.

The Antidote is the best description of a transformational management system I've ever read. Anand and Gary provide a clear roadmap for getting an organization on a growth and market leadership track. The book is readable and understandable, and it accurately portrays the tools and techniques that have been the catalyst for our success at Hubbell.

By replacing traditional approaches with transformation management systems, companies can produce results beyond their expectations. In every area of our company and all parts of our supply chain, reductions in waste and complexity result in lower costs and reliable delivery performance. These competitive advantages, along with our rapid transformation and clear focus and direction, have put Hubbell on the path to becoming the top supplier in the electrical industry.

We've experienced a profound change since we started our transformational management journey with LeanSigma® concepts late in 2001.

In three years, we grew net sales by 54 percent, reduced inventory 53 percent, doubled our rate of innovation, and saved more than 1.5 million square feet of space—benefits we continue to realize and build upon today.

More than eight thousand of our eleven thousand employees have directly participated in this transformation. Applying LeanSigma methods empowers them to be involved in dramatic changes that have lowered the cost of serving our customers while speeding up innovation and new product development.

I can personally vouch for the effectiveness of the holistic approaches Anand and Gary describe. The process has transformed Hubbell and I'm confident it can do the same for your organization...no matter what challenges you face.

Tim Powers
President and CEO
Hubbell Incorporated

Acknowledgments

We are fortunate in our business to work with individuals and organizations that are passionate about continuous improvement and courageous in the journeys they take. Several contributed to this book and we want to thank them for sharing their processes and insights: Barb King and Landscape Structures; Mary Andringa, Glenda Vander Wilt, Kevin Alft and Vermeer Manufacturing; Mel Haught and Pella Corporation; Michael Gerster and WIKA USA; Paul Adelberg and Hayward Pool Products; Tim Powers and Hubbell Inc.; Scott Mitchell and First Data; Art Learmonth and Maytag Services; Michael Hofmann and Sealy; Tom Sween and Deli Express; Harry Schulman and Applica; Fred Heldenfels IV and Heldenfels Enterprises; Teresa Hay McMahon and the Iowa Department of Natural Resources; Sajjan Agarwal and Sigma Electric; Thanasis Molokotos and ASSA ABLOY Americas; Cyndi Leamon and NIBCO; Pat Alexander, Pat Mitchell and Cold Spring Granite; Charles Barrantine and Kodak; David Westgate and Jason Incorporated; Michel David, Inc. - Strategy; T.J. Johnson and Ventana Medical Systems; Ray Stone and Special Metals Wiggin and Dave Jensen and Personalysis Corporation.

We also want to thank all our colleagues at TBM for their inspiration, hard work and dedication to our mission and values and specifically Bob Wenning and Dusty Duckett, senior management consultants, for supplying their valuable perspective on the assessment processes as well as on the Voice of the Customer and value innovation.

Anand Sharma
Gary Hourselt

INTRODUCTION

Unleashing Your Organization's Potential

We understand that you may be feeling squeezed these days. On one hand, you've got urgent demands to improve financial performance—to increase revenues, cut costs, and improve profitability. On the other hand, you're facing new challenges from tough competitors and new players outside your industry and outside the country to get and keep customers.

We see the effects of this growing pressure every day. If not managed properly, it can poison an organization and destroy its ability to compete. Managing the extreme pressures of this new century requires doing business differently, and that can be a scary proposition. The antidote may promise a return to health but it also means you must let go of the unhealthy state your organization currently endures. Letting go of what we know, even when it isn't functioning very well, can cause serious anxiety, so we take it a step at a time. The antidote is not an instant cure-all but a step-by-step transformation, an evolutionary journey to peak performance.

Our cure for pressure—which also helps you apply some pressure of your own—has been developed and refined during decades of work with hundreds of companies. It is the antidote to a way of doing business that is well past its prime. Hierarchical, command-and-control management can no longer survive and thrive in the global marketplace. It's like trying to race against a car on your horse, or against an airplane in your car. You can do everything right and it won't matter.

The extreme challenges of the twenty-first century demand a new way of doing business, a new management system that supports your company's need for speed, agility, quality, innovation, and growth. This *transformational management system* involves everyone in squeezing out waste, adding value to your processes, improving reliability and reducing variability in your processes, learning and responding to customer needs, and developing creative solutions to your—and your customers'—most pressing problems.

This book describes the journey our clients take as they embed the transformational management system in their own organizations, although none takes exactly the same path. As you will see, it all begins with getting your house in order. Every organization wastes time and money every day. Reducing that waste improves quality and productivity, accelerates delivery, reduces costs, and increases customer satisfaction. If that's all we helped organizations do, we would be like most other consulting companies, and we're not. We help you achieve operational excellence by involving your employees in the process. Leaders notice a new energy when this happens. They see pride and joy in the workplace. And they feel it themselves. Their work becomes rewarding again, and fun. You'll hear such discoveries in the words of the leaders we quote throughout this book.

As you get your house in order, new opportunities will emerge. You will free up financial and human resources—not to mention floor space—that can be leveraged for growth. So many companies have been so busy putting out fires for so long, that they've settled for the 2 to 4 percent annual growth that's common for most companies. Our clients pursue 15 to 20 percent growth per year through value innovation, a strategy that involves discovering the voice of the customer and designing innovative products and services that meet customers' stated and unarticulated needs. That, too, is in this book.

In the transformational consulting we do with all types of organizations, we see similar and impressive results from their new journeys: productivity up 15 percent, sales up 20 percent, and profits up 25 percent every year, while lead time is reduced by 90 percent and inventory is down 50 percent.

No matter what your organization does, it, too, can get these results—but not with the old management system. By the time you finish this book, you will come to the conclusion that integrating the transformation management system is the antidote to stagnant or declining performance and extreme competitive pressure.

The journey we will show you has its origins in the concept of "lean" production, which essentially focuses on eliminating waste to achieve the shortest possible cycle time and lead time. Toyota is the world's most effective lean practitioner. We will refer to Toyota in the pages that follow, but we'll also talk about Pella Corporation, Hubbell Incorporated, Hayward Pool Products, First Data Corporation, and a number of other companies, and we'll discuss much more than lean production. Our journey goes far beyond waste and lead time reduction, as you will see, to include the key components of the new transformational management system.

Our approach has evolved from our work experiences before TBM Consulting was formed in 1991, and from our consulting experiences since. At its root are the LeanSigma principles we use today, which combine two of the most powerful, proven, and popular business improvement tools: lean and Six Sigma. While lean uses the power of keen observations to initiate quick actions and achieve results, Six Sigma uses the power of proven statistical tools and disciplined reliance on data to solve complex problems with multiple variables. By combining the speed, teamwork, and strategic focus of lean with the discipline, analytical capability, and variability reduction focus of Six Sigma, our clients have achieved and sustained dramatic results faster.

Like your organization, TBM faces a number of challenges to compete in a global marketplace. While our headquarters is in North Carolina, we have offices in Canada, Switzerland, the United Kingdom, Brazil, Mexico, and China. We understand the anxiety that comes with competing worldwide, as well as the anxiety of having worldwide competitors. Our global perspective gives distance and depth to the journey we outline in this book.

In a way, this book is a travel guide for a new destination. While we can point out the milestones, the forks in the road, and the places you will want to go, your organization will still choose its own path. As Marcel Proust said, "We don't receive wisdom; we must discover it for ourselves after a journey that no one can take for us or spare us."

So here's to discovery, and to the journey, and to the wisdom gained by seeking knowledge and striving for excellence, and to the transformation within your reach. You cannot be spared this journey and there's no time to waste.

Let's get started.

CHAPTER ONE

Transforming Your Management System

In 1967, Steve King wrote his senior year thesis at Iowa State University on an idea he called "continuous play." Instead of populating playgrounds with stand-alone slides, see-saws, and swings, Steve described an innovative approach that connected these activities in an integrated system.

The professor didn't share Steve's vision, awarding his thesis a C+. But the idea didn't go away. In 1971, Steve and his wife, Barb, started Landscape Structures, bringing the concept of continuous play to the marketplace. Ten years later they captured a decade of discovery and learning with the introduction of Playbooster®, the world's first post-and-clamp-based play system featuring slides, climbers, overhead bars, bridges, ramps, tunnels, roofs, and decks configured to the customer's desires.

Kids loved it so much that the idea quickly became the industry standard—which naturally attracted competition. Landscape Structures held onto its leadership position through innovative products your children have probably enjoyed: track ride, corkscrew climber, talk tubes, and slidewinder slide. It was the first to coat benches and tables with

PVC for color and comfort, the first to integrate a shade system into a play structure, and the first to offer a playground safety program for elementary schools.

At the same time, two distinguishing characteristics of Landscape Structures—quality and cost—posed challenges as competition grew. Although their company was ISO certified, Steve and Barb knew they needed better processes to deliver the right equipment at the right price and at the right time.

"We have a whole bunch of parts you can pick from and we configure to your design," said Barb. "We do a lot of community builds where the PTA [Parent Teacher Association] gets volunteers together on a weekend to put equipment together. They've probably been raising money for years, so this is a very celebratory occasion. If the parts aren't ready on that weekend, or if those volunteers are missing a couple of bolts, they can't finish the job. It's not a situation where you want people to get egg on their faces."

Landscape Structures also wanted better control of its costs. Although its products typically lasted longer than those of its competitors, they also cost up to 30 percent more. With the emergence of a half-dozen competitors in the United States, and local and regional manufacturers in Europe and Asia, cost became a distinguishing factor. The potential arrival of Chinese competitors only amplified the pressure.

To compete and grow, Landscape Structures had to change. It had to focus on processes and standardize work without stifling creativity. It had to improve quality while cutting lead time and reducing waste. It had to raise productivity within a team-oriented culture that put people first.

The Kings quickly realized they could achieve none of these things if they continued to do business the same old way. What they did not anticipate was the extent of the changes to come.

THE TWENTIETH CENTURY MANAGEMENT SYSTEM

Most leaders give little thought to the management system by which their company operates. Dividing work by function and grouping people in departments to provide those functions is standard practice, as the columns on any organization chart confirm. Employees specialize in the particular skills needed in finance, operations, human resources, engineering, sales and marketing, and other functions. Such specialization on a grand scale began nearly 100 years ago with Frederick Taylor and his book on scientific management.

Before Taylor, skilled craftsmen drew upon years of learning their trades to decide how to do their jobs. Taylor thought they could do better. He watched how steel workers stretched out the time to do a task because of two fears: the fear of losing jobs if they became more productive, and the fear that working faster would set new levels of performance without increases in pay. He also saw the waste produced by workers who relied on instinct and experience instead of rigorous standards.

Taylor believed that applying the scientific method to management would improve productivity and reduce waste. To prove his theory, he spent years performing time studies, clocking how long it took to do a sequence of actions to determine the most efficient way to complete a task.

He presented his findings in *Principles of Scientific Management*, published in 1911. While many factories embraced this new management model with great success, one man built a business empire upon it: Henry Ford.

Scientific management proved that almost any skilled job could be broken down into steps that unskilled workers could perform. Henry Ford identified the steps required to assemble an automobile and arranged these steps in lines to mass produce Model Ts. But he didn't stop there. To make the assembly line even more efficient, he set it in motion. He started with the production of "magnetos," each of which took one man twenty minutes to assemble twenty-nine individual parts. Ford assigned one worker to each part and installed conveyor belts to bring parts to the line and to move the magnetos from worker to worker until the magnetos were finished. He cut assembly time to thirteen minutes. Further refinements, including raising the height of the line so workers didn't have to bend down for parts, slashed assembly time to five minutes.

Before applying what he learned to Model T production, Ford hired Frederick Taylor to conduct a time study to find the optimal speed for his moving assembly line. It was six seconds per pitch. A worker had six seconds to do his task before the next car arrived on the conveyor, when he performed the same job again. Eighty-four separate steps. Eighty-four workers. The process was so efficient, Ford cut the price of Model Ts from $800 to $300, making automobiles affordable for millions of Americans and inspiring manufacturers in other industries to adopt Ford's methods of production.

Ford quickly learned that his assembly lines were only as efficient as his suppliers permitted: When parts didn't arrive at the factory on time, the assembly line slowed or stopped. He decided to solve the problem with a radical plan: Eliminate the suppliers.

In 1927, Henry Ford opened the Rouge Industrial Center on the Detroit River in Dearborn, Michigan. The River Rouge complex converted raw materials into finished Model Ts and, later, into Mustangs, Thunderbirds, and Fairlanes. It had ninety-three buildings, ninety miles of railroad tracks, twenty-seven miles of conveyors, and 53,000 machine tools. Ford-owned ships delivered iron ore, rubber, and other supplies directly to the plant, where more than 100,000 workers produced upwards of 9,000 new cars a month.

To manage the River Rouge complex and other Ford plants, the Ford Motor Company needed a management system capable of organizing hundreds of thousands of people. The hierarchy it built reflected the specialization of labor practiced on the shop floor by grouping support people into functional areas. Layers of management established policies and procedures to command and control the growing bureaucracy.

This is the dominant management model of the twentieth century. Nearly every large corporation has some version of it, and even smaller companies, such as Landscape Structures, quite naturally adopted it. It's the way companies work. Divide up into functions. Encourage specialization. Leave decision-making to the managers and planning to the leaders because they're the ones getting paid to think.

The scientific management system worked well during the simpler times of Henry Ford's era, when manufacturers could dictate what consumers would buy, when workers were happy just to have a job, and when competitors played by the same rules. While that may describe 1935, it sounds archaic today. Today, consumers decide what they want and when they want it. Workers look for jobs that engage their minds as much as their hands. And competitors look for any edge—better, cheaper, or faster—to succeed in a global marketplace.

The old management system is too rigid, too slow, and too inefficient to support companies that must be flexible, fast, and flat to meet today's challenges. A replacement system is desperately needed. Ironically, the best candidate to replace the old system also grew out of the automobile industry.

THE TWENTY-FIRST CENTURY MANAGEMENT SYSTEM

In the 1930s, the leaders of Toyota Motor Corporation, a small Japanese company that made simple trucks—and made them poorly—visited Ford and General Motors to learn more about assembly lines. They were shocked by what they saw. By controlling the whole value chain, Ford's River Rouge complex was able to shrink the lead time from melting iron to making cars. Assembly lines dedicated to the same types of cars allowed for standardization that improved productivity and quality, so much so that Ford was ten times more productive than Toyota, with quality that was thirty times better. To complicate matters, Toyota didn't serve a large market and couldn't dictate what consumers would buy, which made mass production problematic, and it had nowhere near Ford's financial resources.

World War II made things worse, destroying industries—including Toyota's suppliers—and leaving Japanese consumers with little money to spend. Once again, Toyota's leaders decided to learn from their American counterparts, devoting twelve weeks to studying U.S. production processes. The year was 1950, the year Taylor's scientific management system may have peaked and its successor was born.

When Toyota's president returned from his tour of American plants, he assigned his plant manager, Taiichi Ohno, the task of equaling Ford's productivity. Ohno took the challenge personally, devoting the next twenty years to developing what Toyota called the "poor man's production system."

He began with the fundamentals that Henry Ford had applied to his moving assembly lines:

- Standardizing work
- Continuously improving processes
- Identifying and reducing waste
- Maintaining a clean and orderly workplace
- Developing products with manufacturability in mind
- Managing the supply chain

Ohno focused Toyota's efforts to master these fundamentals on the concept of one-piece flow. Unlike Ford, who pushed cars through the assembly line based on the optimal "scientific" speed, Ohno wanted customer demand to *pull* cars through the line: A customer buys a car and that triggers Toyota to order the production of another car, which triggers an order for a muffler, which triggers an order for one sheet of sheet metal to make the muffler.

One-piece flow became Toyota's driving force to improve quality and productivity because it delivered exactly what Toyota needed. Without Ford's financial resources, it couldn't afford to make cars and hold them as inventory. It couldn't afford quality problems and waste. It needed every employee adding value, finding and fixing problems, adapting quickly to changing customer needs, and improving processes.

The contrast with Ford's approach to workflow could not have been more dramatic. Ford made large batches of the same car at the same time; Toyota's flexible system mingled different makes and models on the same line. Ford managed warehouses full of parts needed to build its cars; Toyota developed a network of suppliers who shipped parts to assembly lines when they were needed. Ford had parking lots packed with new cars waiting to be shipped to dealers; Toyota shipped its cars from the end of

Ford

- Made large batches of same cars at same time
- Managed warehouses full of parts
- Had parking lots packed with new cars waiting to be shipped
- Focused on workers performing single tasks in complex processes
- Organized by functions focused on meeting the demands of the function

Toyota

- Built different makes and models on the same line
- Developed network of suppliers who shipped parts to line as needed
- Shipped cars from line to waiting customers
- Involved workers in continuously improving processes
- Organized by cells focused on meeting the demands of the customer

Table 1-1   A Dramatic Change in Workflow

the assembly line to waiting customers. Ford focused its workers on performing single tasks in a complex process; Toyota involved its workers in continuously improving its processes. Ford organized by functions with each function responsible for meeting the demands of the function; Toyota organized by cell with each cell responsible for meeting the demands of the customer.

Ford became the industry leader with its twentieth century management system. By 1980, Toyota had overtaken it.

In the early '80s, Toyota decided to open its first overseas manufacturing plant in the United States. It approached Ford, the company it admired and had learned so much from, and offered 25 percent of Toyota for $2 billion. Ford declined. Toyota then partnered with General Motors, taking over a plant in Fremont, California, that had been closed in 1982 when it claimed the worst quality and productivity of any GM plant, absenteeism above 20 percent, and a contentious local union.

Toyota reopened the Fremont line in 1984 as New United Motor Manufacturing Inc. (NUMMI). Against GM's advice, it brought back the same union and the same workers. Two years later, NUMMI had higher quality and productivity than any GM plant, absenteeism had dropped to 3 percent, and worker satisfaction was best-in-class.

Toyota continued to improve. By the 1990s, its quality and productivity were each at least 50 percent better than Ford's. In 2004, more than half of the top ten selling cars in the U.S were made by Toyota, and its operating profit was greater than that of Ford, GM, and DaimlerChrysler combined. Today, it is the world's most respected automotive company, according to *Fortune*, and one of the top ten companies of any kind worldwide.

Toyota has achieved and maintained this success because it runs its business differently than Ford or GM, or any other company saddled with a twentieth century management system. But Toyota is not alone. Thousands of companies have turned their fortunes around—or built new fortunes—by replacing their old management system with one similar to Toyota's.

They did it, in most cases, because they had to. The command-and-control, batch-and-queue model worked when demand was overwhelming and indiscriminate, competitors were compatriots and close at hand, money solved most problems, and change was slow. That world is gone. Today, your company must be able to solve your customers' problems with high quality products and services, customized to their needs, delivered when they want them, at a cost they can afford. That's what the new transformational management system, this twenty-first century management system, delivers.

A COOL ALTERNATIVE

When Steve and Barb King decided that Landscape Structures had to improve its processes, their search led them to the system popularized by Toyota and widely known as "lean."

"Our culture here is extremely collaborative, team-oriented, and very flat," said Barb, "and those were things we liked about lean manufacturing. We also wanted to hold onto our entrepreneurial spirit as we got larger. And we were enamored with the improvements we were hearing about."

However, the Kings were not enamored with the idea of calling the process "lean." Instead, they came up with a visionary acronym for the journey ahead: *COOL*. **C**reating and recognizing **O**pportunities to improve, **O**pportunities to grow, **L**earning as we go and loving what we do.

They set off on their COOL journey late in 2000 using proven approaches we will talk about in more detail later in this book, including a self-assessment, "kaizen" breakthrough events, value chain mapping, mistake proofing, standard work, and voice of the customer. Six months later, they had moved from functional groups to cells focused on specific customer segments. Within a year, they had freed up 35,000 square feet of space that Steve used to launch his next great idea, Skatewave, designing and producing modular ramps and rails for skate parks.

They used weeklong kaizen (a Japanese approach to continuous improvement) breakthrough events to analyze and improve critical processes. In one week, a cross-functional team studies the existing process, brainstorms ways to make it better, selects the most promising option, implements that option to change the process, and verifies the improvement. Instead of projects that typically take months to deliver minimal value, kaizen events transform a process in a few days. The transformation doesn't stop there, according to Barb King.

"The whole concept of kaizen is, if this doesn't work, we'll try something else until we find something that does. They know that no idea is a bad idea. That's been powerful in conveying the message that nothing needs to be perfect on the first pass. It gives people the license to dream, to throw out wild ideas, to try things, to take risks and continue to work at making things better. We want to be the first one there, the innovator, and that means you have to accept the position that it may not be perfect the first time—although it will always be safe for kids."

When Landscape Structures started its COOL journey, its lead time from customer order to shipping the product was thirty-seven days, well below the industry standard of ten to twelve weeks. By working toward one-piece flow, it can now ship in five to eight days, despite drastically reducing its inventory. The short lead time has improved quality and productivity, increased flexibility, raised customer satisfaction, boosted sales, and strengthened the company's reputation for innovation.

WHAT THIS MEANS TO YOUR COMPANY

In our work with manufacturers, service companies, healthcare organizations, and government agencies, we have seen them discover this antidote to old-style management. They have realized equally dramatic gains during their journeys to a transformational management system:

- Productivity up 15 percent every year
- Sales up 20 percent every year
- Profits up 25 percent ever year
- Lead time reduced by 90 percent
- Inventory reduced by 50 percent

If you work for a service organization, you might be tempted to discount these last two as manufacturing issues, and they are. But they're also your issues. The time it takes to provide a service to your customers is lead time. Information waiting to be used, whether electronically or on paper, is inventory. An excess of lead time or inventory undermines quality, productivity, and customer satisfaction.

Most service organizations already have some version of a manufacturing management system: the command-and-control model institutionalized by Ford and other industrial giants. Although the new system also has roots in manufacturing, it is also transforming the service organizations that embrace it. Here's one example:

Western Union is the worldwide leader in electronic money transfers, handling more than a million transactions every day. It held its first week-long kaizen event in the spring of 2001and has averaged at least one every month since then. Western Union calls them "million dollar projects" because each event delivers a million dollars—or more—to the company's bottom line.

Western Union is a business unit of First Data Corporation. Scott Mitchell leads the business improvement effort for First Data. At the beginning of each kaizen event, he tells the team and executives who attend the kick-off that they're not looking for incremental improvements. They want to blow up the processes to make sure they're driving customer value in everything they do.

"In the service industry, we institutionalize our inefficiencies and call them standards or regulations," Scott said. "We've got to look at those things and realize they're just waste that we need to eliminate."

WHAT THE TRANSFORMATIONAL MANAGEMENT SYSTEM LOOKS LIKE

No matter what products or services your company provides, no matter whether your company is large like Western Union or smaller like Landscape Structures, you must decide if doing business as usual will enable it to compete and grow, or if a new management system is needed. To help with that decision, we want to introduce the critical characteristics of the transformational management system that we've seen in place in hundreds of companies:

- *They focus on what they can control.* You can't control customer demand or competitor ambitions. You can't control how investors react to your plans and performance. You can't control the cost of labor in China. But if you focus on what you *can* control, the things you cannot will mean less. Take the waste out of your operation. Compel customers to buy more from you because your lead time is shorter, your quality is better, and the value you provide is greater. Cultivate durable relationships with customers, employees, and value chain partners. In Chapter 2, we will show you how to take control, how to achieve operational excellence—and how to get results quickly.
- *They leverage these gains for growth.* Every time you eliminate non-value-added steps and reduce waste in a process, you increase capacity, improve productivity, and cut capital spending. If you had a leveraged opportunity to take your existing management and cost structure and double your business in three years, what would you do? Chapter 3 explains how your company can grow by doing more with less.

- ***They connect the dots to a compelling vision of the future.*** This process differs considerably from the traditional approach. First, it's a shared vision: The leadership team defines a direction that resonates with employees. Second, the process provides a roadmap everyone can follow by translating the vision into objectives and action plans through policy deployment. Third, it achieves the objectives through regular performance reviews that promote accountability and provide support. In Chapter 4, we will walk you through the process that Tim Powers, CEO of Hubbell, describes as "the most effective method I have seen to align the objectives of business units and build consensus to focus our efforts on critical and vital few business objectives."

- ***They listen to customers.*** We think of the old model as looking "inside out," while the new one looks "outside in." "Outside in" means spending time at customer sites, observing how they use your products or services (and those of your competitors), identifying their "pain points," and uncovering unarticulated needs. You use the information you collect to develop innovative solutions to customer problems. We'll explain how to determine what customers' value in Chapter 5.

- ***They introduce new products and services quickly at a significantly lower investment.*** How quickly? You can expect to introduce three to four times more new products and services, three to four times faster than you could under the old management system, and at a lower cost. You get to the market sooner, with more features your customers' desire, and with higher levels of quality, because you're doing it right the first time. Chapter 6 describes how to do this using an approach we call Design for LeanSigma.

- ***They run a different race.*** By achieving operational excellence, a company runs the same race better. By inventing radically differentiated products and services using value innovation concepts that provide radically superior value and low cost, a company runs a different race in which few others can compete. Just think of Toyota's ability to quickly deliver high-quality cars tailored to individual customer requirements, or Dell's innovative channel development that has altered the computer landscape. Both forced competitors to run a different race, to compete on their terms. Both became industry leaders by challenging conventional wisdom and locking in customers through value innovation. We will explore this transformative path in Chapter 7.

- *They execute superbly.* To integrate a new management system, an organization has to change. Roles and responsibilities change. Expectations change. The culture changes. To successfully manage this change, companies must execute their plans day after day, month after month, and year after year. This isn't another "flavor of the month." It's not a short-term commitment. Chapter 8 shows you how to make this new way of operating the new standard work—and how to make it stick.

- *They sustain the transformation.* Michael Gerster is president of the WIKA Instrument Corporation in the U.S. WIKA has been on this transformational journey for more than four years. "I asked myself this morning, "If I wasn't the leader, what would this place look like in three years?'" Michael said. "This new way of thinking has such deep roots now that I believe it will continue. It's clear to the entire organization that we shouldn't return to the way we were before." Chapter 9 explains how companies sustain the energy and urgency that continues to generate breakthrough improvements.

- *They leverage new knowledge and capacity to compete globally.* They do this in two ways. The first and most obvious strategy is to serve customers worldwide. Companies such as Toyota, Dell, Western Union, Hubbell, Landscape Structures, and others we will talk about in this book are challenged by, and rewarded for, competing globally. The second strategy, for those companies still insulated from competition outside the U.S., addresses another definition of "global": Companies strive to provide comprehensive solutions for their customers. Chapter 10 looks at how leading companies are challenging old thinking about the global marketplace, the voice of the customer, value innovation, and education to continuously "raise the bar."

NEW CHALLENGES, NEW MARKETS

In truth, no industry or company can escape worldwide competition. Emerging foreign markets seek the goods and services that consumers in the U.S. and the rest of the developed world enjoy. Someone is going to provide those goods and services. Most likely, they will start locally, and if they do it well there, they will look to provide it here next.

Five years ago, Anand talked to the leaders of a major appliance manufacturer about foreign competition and they laughed. They couldn't see any way companies outside the U.S. could penetrate this market. Shortly after that, the company decided to make appliances in China, but not to sell them there. Chinese companies arose to serve the fledgling market, quickly improving quality to competitive levels. And then they turned their attention to the vast U.S. market. The laughing stopped.

This is what we tell our clients: *If you don't do it globally someone else will, they'll do it well, and then they'll do it here.*

We recommend a global triad strategy to help you establish an integrated "global footprint." The strategy considers the social and economic conditions in three zones:

1. In countries where labor is cheap and other costs are low, such as China and India, you can target making products and components with stable designs that generally serve the lower, "value" price point.

2. In countries where labor and other costs are not as low, but are closer to the mega consuming markets such as Mexico and the countries of Eastern Europe, you can target making products and components with less stable designs that generally serve the middle price point.

3. In countries where costs are high and customers are nearby and quite demanding, such as the United States and the countries of Western Europe, you can target making highly customized products with designs and features that are constantly changing, and with price point and margins that are generally higher.

A global leader creates centers of excellence in each of these zones and in all major parts of the world. One example would be the production of a washing machine: You can get the nuts, bolts, baskets, and knobs from India or China, the motor and control panel—which are somewhat customized but still stable designs—from Mexico, and then assemble and customize each machine in local factories near key markets in the U.S.

Developing such global capabilities positions a company to produce a range of products and services, from very simple to very complex, that meet the unique needs of any market, developed or emerging, anywhere in the world.

We live in an opportunistic time. As millions of people around the world increase their purchasing power, they create new markets for simple goods and services. Young, local companies cut their teeth serving basic local needs before sinking their teeth into the more demanding, and more profitable, needs of mature markets in Europe, Asia, and the United States. While companies in the U.S. frequently cannot compete on price, they can compete—and win—by getting close to customers and solving their problems with the right products and services at the right time.

Doing so requires two things:

First, you need a new approach to managing your company that is lean, agile, and growth oriented.

Second, you need leaders who are passionate about what you do.

PERSONAL AND PASSIONATE LEADERSHIP

Henry Ford was passionate about building cars his employees could afford to buy. He immersed himself in the manufacturing process, working side-by-side with engineers and machine operators to test and improve the moving assembly line. Like every successful entrepreneur, he saw an opportunity and a way to seize it, and then he became personally involved in meeting his customers' needs.

When you think about great American companies, you think of the visionary leaders who found innovative ways to solve common problems.

As those companies matured, the innovators left and their entrepreneurial spirit faded. Markets became saturated with competitors offering roughly the same products and services. The mantra became "new, improved"—small changes to keep up with the competition—rather than "new, new"—innovations customers valued.

Passionate leadership was replaced by professional management. A new generation of leaders sequestered themselves in corner offices to pour over the latest financial reports. Companies became victims of managing by the numbers.

"In North America and Europe, top-notch managers want to work less *in* the business and more *for* the business. I think a lot of the problems we have as leaders come from remaining at the 30,000 foot level," observed Michael Gerster, WIKA USA's president. "Since we've started our lean transition, I've gotten much closer to the shop floor. If I was to describe my relationship to the shop floor in the past, I must say with shame that it was more as a cheerleader, trying to be nice to everybody but not really being part of them. This has changed dramatically.

"Before you can change the world, you have to understand how the world works," Michael said. "You won't get that knowledge through financial reports."

Throughout this book, we will introduce you to leaders like Michael Gerster who have a renewed passion for what they do, fueled by being personally involved in listening to customers and improving the processes that solve customer problems. In the old management model, leaders perched at the top of the org chart could distance themselves from these tasks. That distance kept them from finding the passion for their products and services that drives continuous improvement and sustains growth.

The transformational management system, the antidote for business as usual, creates and strengthens connections: connections with customers, connections with suppliers, and connections with employees. It connects supply with demand. It connects daily activities with strategies and plans. And it connects leaders with processes, products, and services, and with the customers they serve.

That is why the leaders featured in this book value the transformative journeys their companies have undertaken.

As with all journeys, it begins with the first step.

CHAPTER TWO

Pursuing Operational Excellence

The journey from the old management system to the new unfolds in three phases: entry, synchronization, and growth. Each leads logically to the next, but is not replaced, because the value of each phase neither diminishes nor ends.

The goal of the entry phase is to get your house in order. When we talk to leaders about what this means, some tell us that's exactly what they need to survive the crises their companies face. Others think of specific areas that are struggling and could use some help. A third group believes their companies really don't have problems that would lead them to do business differently.

We see no such distinctions. Unless a company has devoted years to eliminating waste in its processes, unless its culture has changed from slow and rigid to fast and flexible, unless it has continuously improved its ability to deliver valued solutions to its customers, its house is not in order. It is missing opportunities to improve quality and responsiveness. It is wasting resources on non-value-added activities. And it is fertile ground for stagnant market share, flat revenues, shrinking profits, and eager competitors.

That doesn't mean this journey is for everybody. Not everyone is ready to put their house in order because doing so demands permanent changes in how you run your business. To show you what we mean, consider the qualities common in organizations that have integrated the transformational management system:

- *Senior leaders are personally involved in the improvement process.* They participate on cross-functional teams in kaizen breakthrough events, devoting one week to improving a key part of one process, and they do this more than once. For example, Mary Andringa, Vermeer Manufacturing Company's president and CEO, was on twelve events in the twenty-four months after Vermeer started its journey. Vermeer is a leading agricultural, construction, environmental, and industrial equipment manufacturing company. The personal involvement doesn't end there, as you will see in Chapter 4. If senior leaders delegate this responsibility, your organization will have trouble with the new management system.

- *Work gets done more efficiently and effectively.* Organizations conduct kaizen breakthrough events that focus teams on dramatically improving all or parts of key processes by reducing waste, improving flow, and adding value. Kaizen breakthrough events last one week start to finish. We will describe how they work later in this chapter. If your organization resolutely resists rapid change and risk-taking, you will have trouble with this new management system.

- *Employees participate in continuous improvement.* Kaizen breakthrough events get people involved, open their eyes to new possibilities, and give them permission to initiate positive change. The new management system relies on a strong and complementary team in which employees are partners in the transformation, as shown in Chapter 3. If your organization holds tight to layers of management and the old command-and-control mentality, you will have trouble with this new management system.

- *The business exists to provide solutions, not to manufacture products or deliver services.* This "outside in" perspective begins and ends with customers. It requires a profound knowledge of what customers' value and how you become indispensable to them through a vision and value proposition no competitors can match, as explained in Chapter 5. If your organization believes that it already knows what your customers want and what they want is what you already produce, you will have trouble with this new management system.

- *They improve—and grow—with no end in sight.* Toyota has been at this for more than fifty years. Its ability to continuously improve quality helped Toyota lead ten of eighteen car and truck categories in a 2005 survey of new vehicle owners by J.D. Power & Associates. In comparison, Ford led in two categories. Some analysts are predicting that Toyota will replace General Motors as the world's largest automaker in 2006. If your organization is happy where it's at, you have no incentive to integrate the new transformational management system.

The motivation to transform your organization can come from several sources. The most obvious is the "burning platform," a situation so serious that "jumping off" the old approach and reinventing the company is the only hope for survival. A second motivator is the emergence of serious threats, such as new or stronger competitors, disruptive technologies or solutions, substitute products and services, and the bargaining power of mega buyers and suppliers.

A third group of companies—probably the largest group—gets by just fine. Their motivation to change starts with senior leaders. They do not stand on a burning platform. They fear no imminent threats. Their companies are profitable, growing icons in stable industries. These senior leaders could continue business as usual and few would complain, which makes their bold leadership even more impressive.

DROWNING IN INVENTORY: HAYWARD POOL PRODUCTS

One such company, Hayward Pool Products, seems an unlikely candidate for serious change. It is the worldwide market leader in swimming pool equipment and supplies. When it started its lean journey in 1999, its business was growing at double-digit rates nearly every year. An eighty-year-old company that always earned more than any competitor, Hayward was running out of space in its plants in North Carolina, Tennessee, and California. It was poised to sign off on a new $8 million facility in Nashville when we first talked to Paul Adelberg, Hayward's vice president in charge of manufacturing at that time.

We convinced Paul to postpone the investment while he visited some of our clients to learn first-hand about the new management model.

"When I observed the transformation that took place, I immediately recognized opportunities beyond my expectations," said Paul. "Our on-time delivery wasn't the greatest. We were drowning in inventory. I saw an opportunity not just to improve quality and reduce labor cost, but also to give customers what they want, when they want it."

Paul proposed converting Hayward to the transformational management system. He explained to his fellow senior leaders that such a conversion involved changing the company's culture. They asked why Hayward should change when it was growing and was the market leader. Paul described the achievements of companies already taking the journey and the bottom-line benefit for Hayward: faster growth without large capital investments. The president and chairman approved.

Hayward moved quickly to apply our antidote, conducting kaizen breakthrough events in all four U.S. plants immediately. We will describe that process, including how Hayward applied it, not only because of its ability to deliver immediate improvements and savings, but also because it drives cultural transformation.

Here's a hint of its value to Hayward: It never built that facility in Nashville. In fact, it's now doing almost four times the volume out of its existing Nashville plant. Teams have identified and addressed nearly 200 quality improvements. Turnover is down from 15 percent in 1999 to less than one percent.

The impetus for these and other improvements throughout Hayward was the kaizen breakthrough event.

DRAMATIC IMPROVEMENTS IN ONE WEEK

Kaizen is a Japanese word that combines two roots: *kai* meaning change and *zen* meaning good, which roughly translates into English as continual improvement. A kaizen breakthrough event is a cross-functional, team-based, rapid-fire, action-packed process for rapid improvement. Hold these events every month, as Hayward has done for more than five years, and you create a culture that values operational excellence.

We introduce senior leaders to this culture by inviting them to experience a kaizen breakthrough event at a company skilled at conducting them. The experience can be shocking. Events focus on the physical transformation of a process within one week. Equipment is moved. Desks are relocated. Unnecessary steps are eliminated. The bias for action compels team members to learn by doing, to test their ideas immediately, to take risks. The mantra is *creativity before capital*: Solve problems simply with the resources at hand, solve them quickly, learn, and improve. The key emphasis during kaizen breakthrough events is *action*. When you combine action and common sense, you always make progress, even if you fail. It is truly a Ready-Fire-Aim culture, where quick and crude is preferred over slow and perfect.

In *The Toyota Way* (McGraw Hill, 2004), Jeffrey K. Liker quotes Fujio Cho, president of the Toyota Motor Corporation:

> "We place the highest value on actual implementation and taking action. There are many things we don't understand and therefore, we ask them why don't you just go ahead and take action, try to do something? . . . By constant improvement, or, should I say, the improvement based upon action, one can rise to the higher level of practice and knowledge."

The transformational management system has a bias for action. Rather than months of meetings that lead to proposals that may eventually be acted upon, this new culture gets things done in weeks, or in one week, or in a couple of days. Instead of stretching projects out to address every possible contingency and problem, the new culture demands action: Make changes, observe, make changes, observe, make changes, observe.

It works whether you make products or sell services or do the work of non-profits and government agencies.

"We're trying to build a culture of continuous improvement," said Teresa Hay McMahon, continuous improvement manager for the Iowa Department of Natural Resources. "Success and failure are equally rewarded, but inaction is penalized."

The contrast with the old way of doing business could not be clearer. Most companies reward success, ignore inaction, and punish failure. As a result, they are slow and risk averse and produce limited, random improvements. They won't stand a chance against the fast, agile, flexible, lean companies that exist—or will exist—in their industries.

The first kaizen breakthrough event a company holds is often a turning point for the organization. Senior leaders involved in the team—we recommend that one-third of the leadership team participate in this first event—witness the power of the process. They see how it energizes people, stimulates creativity, eliminates waste, and improves productivity. Employees recognize leadership's personal commitment to the process and feel valued for their contributions. And everyone involved in the event comes away with new hope for the future of their company and the work they do.

SETTING THE STAGE FOR SUCCESS

To make sure the first kaizen breakthrough event becomes a turning point for the organization, it must unfold under the best conditions. This involves assessing the organization, determining the best areas for kaizen breakthrough events, identifying opportunities for growth, and preparing for the event.

TBM uses an Enterprise Assessment approach to evaluate a company's operational performance and potential for growth. It has two components: the High Performance Assessment and the Operational Excellence Assessment.

The High Performance Assessment evaluates a company's current ability to create and sustain growth, and identifies which of ten critical attributes need to be improved. The assessment addresses the critical areas shown in Figure 2-1, including the clarity of the vision and the organization's capabilities and management system. The goal is to create a virtuous circle of client satisfaction, high employee motivation, and value chain partnerships that produce superior shareholder value.

The second component is the Operational Excellence Assessment, which is a narrower and deeper assessment of the company's processes. It identifies where the waste is that will be targeted and reduced during the lean transformation.

During this assessment, we look for areas in which a kaizen event will make the greatest impact in the shortest time. The focus of these initial events is more on changing the culture and promoting learning than on their benefits to the bottom line, although such benefits always emerge. We stack it for success so people will see its value.

Figure 2-1 High Performance Assessment Concept

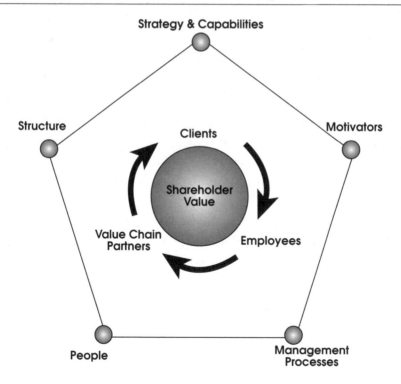

Working with senior leaders, we develop a roadmap for the next six months that shows what the planned kaizen breakthrough events will address. We begin with creating a value chain map of the first area of focus to show its current state, and then involve management in developing a future-state map. A value chain map displays current material and information flow from the customer through your organization to the supply base. Visualizing the process this way reveals disconnects, unnecessary steps, and other opportunities, and helps establish project priorities. The creation of a future-state value chain map establishes a vision for what you want the process to be.

The next step is to begin thinking about what to do with the large resource pool that will be created by kaizen breakthrough events and other improvement activities. Eliminating waste frees up resources you can use to grow your business. For example, when Hayward held its first kaizen breakthrough event, the process to be improved required eight people. By the end of the week, the new process only needed five people.

"From the beginning, we made it public to the entire organization that we would not lay off a single employee due to our kaizen events," said Paul Adelberg. "It's the company's responsibility to grow, to find meaningful work for people. We've never had an employee laid off because of lean activity."

Although the focus of the first phase of the transformation is on operational excellence and the last phase is on growth, the plans for growth need to be outlined early to take full advantage of the resources you will reclaim.

To prepare for the first kaizen breakthrough event, we hold a three-day launch meeting for fifteen to twenty managers, including those in the areas that will be affected by the event, to introduce the process. On the last day, the operations and technical teams figure out which specific area to focus on, select the cross-functional team, set the objectives for the week, arrange logistics, identify who will support the event, and determine how it will be communicated.

The best project areas have a product or service line focus, serve a strategic business need, and have large improvement potential. One-third of the team of eight to ten people work the process, one-third come from support areas, and one-third are outsiders who have nothing to do with the area. Team members commit to being totally involved in the week-long event, full time, no distractions. After the event, the team members who work the process own the process and have more knowledge and tools to continuously improve it.

A key element in the preparation is getting people ready for its immediate impact. The event will last just one week and it will lead to action, often to a radically new—and better—process. The goal of the kaizen breakthrough event is not to make recommendations but to physically change the process to eliminate waste right away. That's a shock to a slow-moving organization.

IMMEDIATE IMPROVEMENT: THE KAIZEN BREAKTHROUGH EVENT

Two years into leading his organization, WIKA USA President Michael Gerster decided it was time to learn about lean. WIKA, the number two manufacturer of pressure instruments in the United States, faced a common challenge to mature industries: products that haven't changed much in decades becoming commodities distinguishable only by price. Michael knew WIKA had to become more agile to make the company and its products more valuable to its customers.

Paul Adelberg at Hayward Pool Products had invited Michael to participate in a public kaizen event. When Michael called Paul to find out more about Hayward's lean journey, Paul confided that he had been doing manufacturing for thirty-five years and wasn't ashamed to admit that they hadn't done the obvious until they started doing kaizen.

"I said, 'Here we go. We're coming,'" Michael remembered. "I reserved four spots at the kaizen event and went with my technical director who's now the COO, a newly-hired industrial engineer who's now our kaizen leader, and the production manager who's now the head of manufacturing. We went through the one-week process. On Friday we hopped into a taxi and I didn't say a word. Those three guys immediately made the transition to what was in it for their daily jobs. They saw answers to questions they'd been asking all along.

"We were on fire," Michael said.

Michael asked TBM to assess WIKA. "I learned later that the assessment is not just to get ready for the transition, but to see if the leaders are serious about sustaining change," Michael said. "Evidently, we passed."

WIKA decided to focus the first kaizen events on lead time for some key product lines, which was at four to six weeks. Attacking lead time involved improving flow, which would improve quality and productivity and reduce inventory. Kaizen breakthrough teams eventually bent twenty-three individual product lines into U-shaped cells, redistributing the work and implementing one-piece flow. They cleaned out inventory and improved productivity 15-20 percent in each area.

"The results of the first kaizen event were breathtaking. They shook the organization to its foundation," said Michael. "It immediately pulled the entire leadership team over. Everybody understood they'd better get on this train or they're going to get run over."

Weeklong Kaizen breakthrough events are so effective—and so shocking—because physical changes are made to critical processes that have been running the same way for years or even decades. The bias for action compels teams to finish the week with a significantly better process than the one they started with on Monday. Where "slow and elegant" ruled the day, we push for "quick and crude." Where months of studies led to recommendations of huge investments, we encourage "creativity before capital." Act. Simplify. Innovate. Flow.

This is what happens during a typical kaizen breakthrough event for any type of process:

Monday: Conceptual training on the transformational management system, kaizen breakthrough methodology, and standard operations; identify areas of initial focus.

Tuesday: Analyze the current process; formulate process improvements; physically make the improvements to implement one-piece flow; make safety and workplace organization improvements.

Wednesday: Continue hands-on improvement; re-time the process; make major equipment moves, if necessary; make fixtures, tools, and other enhancements.

Thursday: Refine the improvements; run trials on the new, improved process under actual production conditions; establish standard work; run and re-time the improved process; document the new standard operation.

Friday: Present the results to the senior management team and celebrate.

Deli Express held its first kaizen breakthrough event in its delivery trucks. The company delivers fresh sandwiches daily to more than 23,000 convenience stores in twenty-six states. The first event saved one hour for every driver, every day. A second kaizen event focused on what to do with that hour to grow sales. The kaizen team created a small box and a script. The box holds sample products from lines a store doesn't carry, such as bakery products. Using the script, the driver offers free treats when he drops the box off, and then stops back the following week to see what the manager thinks. In the first seven months of using the box and script, direct store sales grew 10 percent.

"After that first event we realized that we have 300 people in the field and they're all doing things their own way," said Tom Sween, president of EA Sween Company, which manufactures and distributes Deli Express. "We've been trying to standardize ever since." In January 2003, the company brought all 300 territory sales managers to the Minneapolis Convention Center to zero in on what happens from the time they turn off the key at the store to the time they turn on the key to leave. Using seven trucks brought in for the event, the managers experimented with shelving, carts, and sequences of steps. By the end of the week they had created standards for everyone to follow that all managers had practiced.

Deli Express has conducted more than 100 kaizen events in three years with its field force, in its plants, and on business processes. Before its first kaizen event, sales were relatively flat. It's had double-digit growth ever since.

KAIZEN BREAKTHROUGH FOR BUSINESS PROCESSES

The kaizen breakthrough event is equally effective for service or business processes. While its roots are in manufacturing, its purpose is process improvement, and it doesn't matter what kind of process needs to be improved.

Take the Iowa Department of Natural Resources, for example. The agency held its first kaizen breakthrough event in June 2003 at the urging of the Iowa Coalition for Innovation and Growth—although "urging" may be too mild a word.

The coalition of business leaders, formed to address areas in which business can make a difference, surveyed its members to identify the top regulatory barriers. The number one barrier was air quality new source construction permits. The DNR's Air Quality Bureau issues about 2,000 new source construction permits a year. It took sixty-two days to issue a permit, which frequently delayed construction, and the backlog of applications frustrated efforts to speed it up.

Members of the coalition approached the DNR to underscore the problem and propose a radically different solution: a free kaizen event. Their only condition was that the department had to agree to use the event to attack waste in the permitting process.

The DNR drafted twenty people, one-third of them customers of the permit process, for its first kaizen breakthrough event. The team discovered a very complex process. "Business processes are invisible," said Teresa Hay McMahon, continuous improvement manager for the Iowa DNR. "Our experience has been that the processes we tackle have been large, complex, not standard, and not tightly focused on quality, cost, and time. We started where we had the most pain."

They started fast. By the end of the first kaizen event, a process that had taken sixty-two days now took just twelve. Six months later, the backlog of 600 applications had been eliminated, and the lead time was down to six days to get a permit. That's when the coalition returned to encourage the DNR to hold more events.

The second event in the spring of 2004 focused on clean water construction permits. The DNR provides the permits for Iowa cities to upgrade their water treatment facilities and, through the Iowa Finance Authority, the low-interest loans that the cities need to fund them. The event focused on the permitting side, but also affected the state financing side. Cities were going to other lenders and paying higher rates because it was easier than working with the state. That meant less money coming back into the state revolving fund used for clean water projects.

Members of the finance side participated in the kaizen breakthrough event. The team's pre-work determined that it took eighteen months to issue a permit. Once the kaizen event started, the team discovered the lead time was more like twenty-eight months. By the end of the week, that had been shortened to four-and-a-half months, which included a mandatory thirty-day public comment period. The number of steps was nearly cut in half and the number of handoffs dropped from forty-three to nineteen.

One year later, the Iowa Finance Authority reported an increased number of applications for funding water treatment facility construction.

"In the past, the attitudes of many regulatory customers who came to us ranged from cynical to hostile," said Teresa. "Kaizen has completely changed these relationships. During the last legislative session, we heard from several legislators that their constituents were telling them it's becoming easier to do business in Iowa. We saw a memo to the governor of Nebraska. The writer wanted to know what's going on in Iowa and why he couldn't do it in Nebraska."

The DNR has taken the lead in communicating the value of our antidote, the transformational management system, and conducting kaizen events with other agencies—thirty at last count, including one for the Department of Corrections on offender reentry into the community. While the event reduced delays by 90 percent, the real focus was on the transition.

"I saw the director recently and he said they've changed the mindset of offenders because they are talking about preparing to leave from the day they walk into the facility," said Teresa. "And that's because of kaizen."

FINDING AND REMOVING WASTE

Think for a moment about a process that is important to you. It may be a process for selling your products or services or reviewing your group's performance or reporting financial results, or it may be another process that dictates how successful your organization is. Pick one, think for a moment about when that process starts and when it ends, and estimate what percent of the time from start to finish is wasted.

Here's what we mean by wasted time:

- *Defective products or services.* The cost of repair, rework, scrap, replacement, inspection, warranty claims, etc.
- *Overproduction.* Making anything during the process that someone has not ordered.
- *Excessive inventories.* The "extra" produced by the process that has to be moved and stored, that hides defects and other problems, and that causes long lead times and obsolescence.
- *Unnecessary processing.* Steps in the process that seem like they add value but aren't needed.
- *Unnecessary transportation.* Making stuff one place and then hauling it to another floor or another facility—or storing it—for the next step.
- *Waiting.* People don't have any work to do, or they're waiting for someone—a supplier or another employee/department upstream in the process—to give them work, or they're watching a machine do the work.
- *Excessive motion.* The wasted movements that employees must make to perform their work that are ergonomically incorrect or cause fatigue.

With these types of waste in mind, what percentage of your process do you think is totally unnecessary? This is what we have found: As much as 95 percent of the time in any process is wasted time. The experiences of the Iowa DNR are a good example. The lead time for air quality new source construction permits was cut from sixty-two days to six, eliminating 90.33 percent of wasted time. The clean water construction permit time was cut from twenty-eight months to four-and-a-half months, with one of those months devoted to a mandatory public comment period, eliminating 87 percent of wasted time. Delays in the offender reentry process for the Department of Corrections were reduced by 90 percent. It doesn't matter what the process is, most of the time it takes does not add value.

The goal is to reduce processes to their core values, eliminating steps that don't add value, and retaining only those steps that do add value. When you do this, you dramatically reduce lead time, which profoundly improves quality, responsiveness, and customer satisfaction; lowers costs; and generates new enthusiasm and team spirit.

After three years of working on its key processes, Hayward Pool Products closed a 240,000-square-foot plant by creating space for its activities in two other plants. One of those plants also became home for two new acquisitions. Hayward has doubled the business from one of those acquisitions in just two years. Nobody has been laid off because of its lean activities. Nearly 80 percent of employees have participated in at least one kaizen breakthrough event, and some have been involved in ten to fifteen such events.

"Almost across the board, there isn't anyone who participates in kaizen programs who doesn't end up being better for it, smarter, learning better techniques, learning to work smarter," said Paul Adelberg. "I think there would be an uprising if we suggested going back to the way we did it before."

Customers would join the uprising: Hayward has gained ten market share points since it started its lean journey.

AN ONGOING FOCUS ON ELIMINATING WASTE

A kaizen breakthrough event finds and removes waste in one week, but the streamlining doesn't stop there. As people work the new process, backlogs and excess inventory are pared down. Enthusiastic employees start to view the process through "kaizen eyes," noticing opportunities for improvement that were hidden in plain sight before people knew how to observe.

Simpler issues or projects with a narrow focus may be the target of a *point kaizen*, an abbreviated one- to three-day kaizen event that also involves a cross-functional team. Companies use point kaizens for such areas as removing a bottleneck in a key process, identifying and eliminating the causes of a high error rate, and resolving an item from an earlier kaizen week.

For example, Hayward recently used a point kaizen to improve its process for creating operator manuals for its equipment. The process typically took six to eight weeks. The point kaizen team worked for three days to get the length of the process down to one week.

Another formal approach for training middle managers and supervisors to eliminate waste is called Managing for Daily Improvement, or MDI. Typically, six to eight individuals within a department receive training in two-hour modules on the key concepts that will help them eliminate waste, improve flow, and manage the improvement process on a daily basis. For each concept, they identify an area to apply what they learned during another two-hour period. They repeat this process for every concept, learning within a week not only a new concept, but also how to apply it in their jobs.

Pella Corporation, a leading manufacturer of windows and doors, has quadrupled its sales since embarking on its lean journey in 1992. Pella conducts MDI training for its managers. Each manager devotes one to three hours per day to MDI activities concentrated in a specific area such as standard work, visual management, or 5S. (We will discuss these areas in Chapter 8.) Managers report on their progress at the end of the cycle, which is typically one month. Every year, each department manager owes the company 2,000 hours in savings from his or her MDI efforts.

Landscape Structures encourages individuals and department teams to identify and pursue MDI projects. The company has MDI project criteria and a standard format for reporting out. "This has been as powerful as kaizen for us," said Barb King. "Kaizen is like a rifle strike. MDI becomes your way of doing business."

OPERATIONAL EXCELLENCE MUST COME FIRST

The first phase of the transformational management system is to get your house in order, to develop a culture that will not tolerate waste in any form, in any process. To give you an idea of how Phase I of the transformation can benefit your organization, consider the gains made by Hayward Pool Products when it jettisoned its old management system:

- Injection mold press set-up times down from eight hours to one hour.
- Mold changeovers from 45 per week in one plant to 235 per week.
- Work-in-progress (WIP) inventory at one plant down from $2.7 million to $900,000.
- Another plant's WIP reduced from $4.2 million to $1.3 million.
- WIP inventory turns up from 12.6 to 40 times per year.
- On-time delivery improved from 65 to 70 percent to 93 percent.
- Time to market for new products reduced by 50 percent.
- All managers in all plants have participated in kaizen breakthrough events.
- Two-thirds of hourly employees have participated in kaizen breakthrough events.
- Productivity, as measured by sales per employee, improved from $202,000 to $319,000.
- Another productivity measure: Each employee at one plant was producing 5.9 units per day and is now turning out 8.3 units.
- Turnover down from 15 percent to less than one percent.
- Lower workers' compensation rates.
- Business grown by 50 percent with no change in direct labor headcount.
- Doubled the business while closing a 240,000-square-foot facility.
- Gained ten market share points.

While each of these gains is impressive, it's the combination that sets Hayward apart. It grew the business significantly without having to hire more people or build new facilities. It improved productivity at the same time it improved employee satisfaction. It dramatically accelerated key processes and reduced inventory, while gaining market share. In other words: *In every area of the company, on every measure by which Hayward evaluates its success, the company made significant improvements, once it set off on its lean journey.*

And that's just the payoff for Phase I!

There comes a point during this phase when the focus begins to turn from inside the organization to outside of it. Nearly all key processes depend on suppliers on the front end and customers, dealers, and/or distributors on the back end to improve flow. As you get your house in order, issues with supply and demand surface and must be addressed to continue the transformation.

Here's one example. We worked with a company that had drastically reduced its lead time and wanted to turn its newfound responsiveness into a competitive advantage. The company approached dealers and outlets about ordering and receiving their products on a daily basis instead of monthly so the dealers and outlets wouldn't have to store inventory on their shelves. When they balked at the added cost of sending out trucks every day, the company said it would absorb the cost: Just give us your order by 10 p.m., and we'll ship it to you the next day, and you'll know when it's coming because the route will be predictable. Most customers couldn't resist the offer. As they took their inventories down, they relied more and more on the company to supply them—and bought less and less from its competitors. At the same time, the daily demand improved the flow of products through the company because they were now being built to specific, daily orders.

The initiation of Phase II typically begins one to two years after you have started Phase I, although some areas may be ready for it in just six months. Phase II focuses on synchronization through supply/demand chain alignment and listening to the voice of the customer. We will explore these elements later in the book.

The dramatic improvements made in Phases I and II free human and capital resources that can be used to fuel growth. We advise all of our clients to communicate to their employees, early and often, that no one will be laid off because of the improvements that will be made. This can be a hard promise to keep when up to 95 percent of every key process is being eliminated.

Phase III involves translating the voice of the customer through value innovation into new products and services that serve markets you're not supplying and customer needs you're not serving. If your company is in a mature industry and you are growing at the industry rate, which is typically 2 to 4 percent, and if your productivity improves 10-15 percent a year, you need to grow three to five times faster than your industry to keep your people gainfully employed. We want to accelerate the product/service development process to leverage the gains made during Phases I and II. This will build brand loyalty, lock in customers, and increase market share.

The next five chapters describe how to do this, beginning with the agents of change: people and leadership.

RIDING A SEA CHANGE

On Friday, the last day of the Iowa DNR's second kaizen event, one of the team members reporting on the week's achievements described himself as "whip-smart." Anyone who has ever taken a risk or initiated a change and been disciplined by the organization can relate to the term. You have to be "whip-smart" to survive and that means no risks, little change, and a well-cultivated negativity about anything new.

"Whip-smart" leaders, managers, and employees will resist the antidote of the new management system. They can be won over. They can unlearn the whip and recapture the desire to do better that caused them problems in the first place. Teresa Hay McMahon has seen it.

"It's amazing when you look at what's happening here," she said. "We've had a lot of conversions on the road to kaizen, people who come into kaizen breakthrough events as complete cynics and can't imagine success. They've survived every flavor of the month. They come out believing in our mission, knowing they can take risks and make changes. We've never seen this. We've had a sea change."

CHAPTER THREE

Choosing Your Organization's Path

La Cage aux Sports was the largest sports bar and restaurant chain in Quebec in 1998 with more than forty locations and sales around $65 million. Sales had stabilized at that level, however, trends had started to drift in the wrong direction, and the bars and restaurants were losing the "buzz" of popularity.

The company's CEO enlisted the help of our strategic consulting affiliate, Michel David, Inc. - Strategy of Montreal, to turn things around. Michel David, Inc. - Strategy started with an assessment that revealed that a number of decisions, large and small, had pulled the bars and restaurants off course. Working with the CEO, Michel David, Inc. - Strategy planned a series of high-impact projects to get La Cage aux Sports back on track:

- Define and develop a high-performance organization aligned to the key success factors in the restaurant trade.
- Clarify a differentiated strategic position.
- Align the business model and profitability disciplines.
- Redefine human resource policies to become the "employer of choice."

- Act on a bar strategy that included reinventing supplier relationships.
- Develop and pursue an optimum penetration strategy for current markets.
- Evaluate major opportunities for diversification.

The company restated its market position as "sports, gang, fun," and hatched a metaphor to keep everyone on track: the egg. Anything that was "sports, gang, fun" was in the yolk. Anything clearly related to the yolk was in the white and OK. Everything not in the egg was excluded.

Five years after redefining the company, sales for La Cage aux Sports had reached $90 million and its value had tripled. Its journey illustrates the foundational elements that need to be addressed early in any transformation: a clear mission and vision, an enlightening snapshot of the current condition of the organization, a commitment to operational excellence, a plan for leveraging lean for growth, shared accountability for success, and the right people in the right positions. These things all need to be in place for the antidote to work.

THE FORK IN THE ROAD

A cultural transformation is not a revolution brought about by a discontented mass of employees, but a revolution stirred by the company's leaders. It starts with a vision that creates the excitement and urgency within the organization that will be the catalyst for change. The new culture focuses on customers, values speed and innovation, demands quality, and recognizes that employees are partners in achieving your goals. The mission and vision should reflect these characteristics.

They should also be clear and succinct. We encourage our clients to take a lean approach to this: Involve senior management in developing a *mission* (purpose), *vision* (direction), and *values* (mission/vision brought to the daily work level) that employees can identify with and leaders can use to drive behavior. Develop them within a day or less. All you are looking for is a framework for what comes next.

That doesn't mean you take these guiding precepts lightly. To lead change, leaders must be able to imagine what is possible and connect the dots from here to there. There are seven essential qualities of a vision that rallies people to pursue a better future:

1. *It has to be crisp.* Clear. Concise. Simple.

2. *It has to be compelling and exciting.* People care about how it will help the organization and society, but they also want to know how it supports their security, family, and obligations. And it has to be exciting to keep everyone enthusiastically involved in the transformation.

3. *A roadmap deploys it.* People need to know how they will personally contribute to achieving the vision. They need to know how to connect the dots, too.

4. *Leaders must communicate it.* The most effective communication is honest, often, and personal. Leaders need to be honest about where the organization is, the challenges ahead, and how you will meet them. They must communicate this personally in as many forums and through as many avenues as possible.

5. *Rewards must align with it.* Employees must clearly see how behavior that supports the vision will be rewarded.

6. *Support must be present to achieve it.* Employees need the right tools and training to do their jobs well. They also need to be in the right jobs.

7. *Obstacles must be removed.* Leaders have to reexamine the policies, procedures, and performance measures that may keep people from moving in the right direction.

Ventana Medical Systems' vision is "Experience Ventana." Founded in 1985, the company focuses on tissue and the management of chemical reactions on glass slides used to diagnose cancer and other diseases. In 2004, Ventana made *Fortune* magazine's list of "100 Fastest Growing Companies in the U.S." *BusinessWeek* ranked it number eighty-one on the magazine's "100 Hottest Growth Companies for 2005" list. Both lists reflect sales and earnings growth. Ventana grows 20-25 percent per year by taking lean to its customers through its complete lean laboratory solutions and customer care philosophy, or "Experience Ventana."

"Our message to our customers is about moving beyond what is, the batch lab, to what can be, the lean lab," said T.J. Johnson, senior vice president of corporate development and manufacturing operations. "It's about experiencing the lab of the future." Ventana's marketing and sales people visit customers' labs to help them become more efficient using tools like value chain mapping and work-flow analysis. They lock customers in by selling solutions: diagnostic solutions that provide more information about the cause and treatment of disease, workflow solutions that bring lean thinking to the lab, and a customer care infrastructure that is the best in the industry.

"We have competitors that do pieces of what we do well, but none can do it all," said T.J. "As long as we provide the total solution, it makes it extremely difficult for customers to justify buying a competitor's less-costly instrument when they know they give up better delivery, better customer care, better access to diagnostics—they give up the whole solution. That's a huge competitive advantage for us. Couple it with our world-class innovation engine in R&D and world-class sales organization, and we're not just bringing solutions, we're bringing solutions that hold up under stress and pressure."

CHOOSING THE BEST PATH

Ventana's vision reflects its leaders' knowledge of the external and internal factors that will shape its future. It begins with an exceptional understanding of how its customers' work beyond how they use Ventana's products. The vision is not to be the product leader, but the solutions leader. To move toward that vision, Ventana must be so close to its customers that it understands their needs better than the customers do. Such understanding is personal and experiential and requires senior managers to walk in their customers' shoes often to uncover unarticulated needs and unique insights. We challenge the leaders we work with to spend at least one week every month on the ground with customers.

The second key factor affecting the vision is leadership's connection with people at all levels of the organization. Approaches for making and maintaining contact with employees may include regular all-employee meetings, participation in department meetings, columns in company newsletters, regular e-mail or voicemail messages, having lunch with employees, and being visibly involved by walking around often and unannounced.

Other key factors include the external environment—leaders must be brutally honest about the competition, markets, economic conditions, and other factors they have no control over; the potential of the organization based on its traditions and on the creativity and potential of people at all levels; and a culture free of fear, where people feel they can be honest without being punished for it.

The best way to determine how well your organization is positioned to act on a compelling vision is to evaluate your current state of affairs and set some short- to medium-term goals. We do this through a comprehensive Enterprise Assessment.

WHERE DO WE START?

No matter what your organization does, the number of areas that seriously need immediate improvement can seem overwhelming—and that doesn't include the problems hidden from sight. You can't work on everything at once, which means you need a process for identifying and prioritizing the areas to improve. We begin with an Enterprise Assessment, which has two parts:

1. The High Performance Assessment, which we learned from Michel David, Inc. - Strategy, evaluates your ability to create and sustain growth by documenting the current performance and mindset of your people and identifying the gaps to reach your strategic vision.

2. The Operational Excellence Assessment identifies waste and operational improvement opportunities to become a responsive, high-qual-

ity solution provider through the development of detailed current and future state value stream maps.

The process for identifying and prioritizing areas to improve concludes with two additional steps:

3. Develop a Go Forward work plan and Cultural Transformation Plan, and determine projected costs and payback.

4. Discuss results to gain buy-in from management and determine the next steps together.

Documenting Current Performance and Mindset: The High Performance Assessment

A valid assessment depends on asking the right questions. Our approach is to have a representative sample of employees respond to questions about the company's competitive and organizational strength and its economic performance. We analyze the responses, which include comments, to identify emerging issues to be discussed. We then validate that analysis through face-to-face interviews with key people.

The questions fall into ten categories and capture the best practices of leading growth companies identified by Michel David, Inc. - Strategy. To get a sense of the current condition of your organization, we ask the respondents to take a few minutes to rate their perceptions on each of the following characteristics using a five-point scale:

1 = Do not agree
2 = Somewhat agree
3 = Mildly agree
4 = Agree
5 = Strongly agree

A score of 4.0 or higher indicates superior performance. We rarely see a score that high on any characteristic on a first assessment. A score of 3.5 to 3.9 is considered "good," and even this is unusual on many characteristics during the first assessment.

Key Characteristics	Rating

Strategy

- Clear advantage over competitors   _____
- Successful strategy implementation   _____
- Unique market position   _____
- Understanding market and needs   _____
- Understanding competitors   _____
- Know how to double volume   _____

Client-Driven

- Customer is always right   _____
- Differentiated offering in each segment   _____
- Among top suppliers of strategic clients   _____
- Win-win relationships   _____
- Best client knowledge   _____
- Management spending time with customers   _____

Innovation

- Introduction of new products/services   _____
- Improvement of business relations   _____
- Recognized as the most innovative   _____
- Active support of entrepreneurship   _____
- Assessment of customers' needs   _____
- Processes to identify business opportunities   _____
- Processes to exploit business opportunities   _____

Operational Excellence

- Operational excellence led by senior management   _____
- Continuous productivity gains   _____
- Quick problem solving   _____
- Results on time, on budget   _____
- Chooses best product or service   _____
- Effective product management   _____
- Least cost producer   _____

Leadership

- High standards promoted   _____
- Competent management   _____
- Strategic alignment of daily activities   _____
- Fact-based discussions   _____

Key Characteristics	Rating

Leadership

- Employees trust management _____
- Clear strategy _____
- Internal politics not tolerated _____

Structure

- Clear responsibility and accountability _____
- Lean organization _____
- Structure supports competitive advantages _____
- Units receive requisite support _____
- Enough attention to each market segment _____
- Simple coordination _____

Management Processes

- Internal communication supports changes _____
- Performance managed against priorities _____
- Effective planning _____
- Best idea wins _____
- Resource allocation aligned with strategy _____
- On-time decision making _____
- Disciplined follow-up process _____

People

- Highly talented people in pivotal jobs _____
- Required expertise to execute strategy _____
- Retain best people _____
- Hiring introduces superior people _____
- Zero tolerance for lack of performance _____
- Disciplined people development _____

Motivators

- Satisfactory working conditions _____
- Challenging assignments _____
- Recognition of achievement _____
- Constructive performance evaluations _____
- Clear definition of job expectations _____
- Pay fair for all _____
- Employees have required resources to execute _____

Key Characteristics	Rating
Performance Indicators	
• Employees satisfied	____
• Shareholders satisfied	____
• Customers satisfied	____
• Superior growth performance	____
• Superior profitability	____
• Superior financial return	____

Table 3-1 The High Performance Assessment

For example, the average scores for *operational excellence* on the first High Performance Assessment for a manufacturing company that is an industry leader were:

- Operational excellence led by senior management = 3.4
- Continuous productivity gains = 3.2
- Quick problem solving = 2.7
- Results on time, on budget = 2.7
- Chooses best product or service = 2.7
- Effective product management = 2.4
- Least cost producer = 1.7

Relevant comments provided by the respondents—and included in the report to the company's leaders—helped clarify the scores:

- "Least cost producer? In most cases, we are the highest. Our gross margin is not as good as others in the industry. We give more discounts to dealers. Too much design engineering support of our existing products adds to our overhead costs."
- "Our new product project management is rarely delivered on schedule with acceptable levels of quality. Some projects I have been involved with have lacked leadership."

- "Quick problem fixing? We need much more focus on operational problems. We are reactive; we need to be more proactive in this area. We are slow in accepting there is a problem."
- "Productivity gains? They are showed on paper, but we have a terrible time with the sustainment of new procedures and initiatives. Our current measurements are questionable."

The next step is to look for a pattern in the highest and lowest scores. The company in this example scored highest in "satisfactory working conditions" and "challenging assignments," but scored low in "zero tolerance for lack of performance" and "internal politics not tolerated." People were happy to work there, but didn't feel totally accountable for results. Respondents commented that "we not only tolerate a lack of performance, we encourage it by failing to address problems," and "it's not what you know, it's who you know." The company made accountability for results a priority and used policy deployment, which we will discuss in the next chapter, to review performance regularly and help underperforming areas meet their goals.

The company chose to ignore its lowest scoring characteristic—least cost producer—because it competed on value and innovation and not on cost.

The scores and comments can also be used to clarify the competitive situation, match strengths to opportunities, and determine if the organization's culture will support change.

We look at three elements of an organization's competitive position: whether the industry and future environment are predictable; whether the organizational culture is visionary, rational, or disparate; and how strong it is compared to competitors.

We also analyze the framework for change beginning with the amount of change required compared to the organization's normal behavior (proactive or reactive). The results on four statements in the questionnaire illuminate cultural readiness for change: trust in management; best idea wins; zero tolerance for non-performance; and fact-based discussions.

The assessment and analysis inevitably open the eyes of leaders who naturally assume they know their organizations and understand the issues to be addressed. "Before the assessment, we had assumptions about what we were doing and how our people really thought of us, but we had no way to quantify it," said Pat Mitchell, retiring president and COO of Cold Spring Granite. "The assessment was a shock. It showed us that we're too internally focused and, because our culture is risk-averse, we're too slow to respond."

That was five years ago. Acting on the assessment, Cold Spring Granite challenged its assumptions about customer needs, its standards for delivery, the threat of global competition, and the company's ability to grow, and used kaizen breakthrough events and other improvement tools to change the culture and redefine the company.

"The biggest thing we're dealing with now is foreign competition," said Pat. "We're having to convert to being a distributor. I tell our people the only thing that's going to be left for us to make is stuff that's needed instantly, and it's even better if it's complex. That's what will be left for us, and that's a monstrous change in our company. Our entire focus used to be on quarrying and manufacturing. Now we have to become more of a distributor, while at the same time finding the niches left for our manufacturing."

The transformation of Cold Spring Granite from manufacturer to manufacturer/distributor and from internally focused and slow, to customer-focused and fast began with its first assessment. As Pat concludes, "The assessment rocked the culture of the company. We looked into the mirror and saw not just what we needed to change, but how to accomplish it. We're now able to identify root causes for why our growth strategies have not been successful and what we need to do to change that. It's energized us."

Picturing the Present and Future:
The Operational Excellence Assessment

TBM typically conducts Operational Excellence Assessments for its clients over the course of one week. Before the week starts, we ask the leadership team to give us a sense of their business by: (1) documenting current performance; and, (2) describing their company.

The documentation takes the form of one page of metrics on sales, quality, inventory, market share, and other key indicators showing recent trends and projected performance.

The description focuses on basic product/service families and includes such information for each family as the number of people working on it, sales, whether it is strategic, and if it is growing.

The first order of business when we arrive on site is a two-hour presentation by the senior person and his or her management team to introduce what products or services they offer, how they go to market, who their customers are, how business is progressing, and what they need to do to drive improvement. After the presentation, we walk through the facility to get a sense of how the organization operates and what opportunities are evident. We're on the lookout for such things as excess inventory, flow or the lack of it, and people working or walking around.

We reassemble the management team and engage team members in a value stream mapping exercise. A value stream map is a visualization tool that shows the flow of materials and information from suppliers through the organization's processes to end customers. You can create a value stream map for any product or service your organization delivers, whether it is playground equipment, pressure gauges, insurance forms, new construction permits, or patients in a medical center.

A high-level value stream map helps everyone see the major activities that occur to produce and deliver products and/or services. It reveals obvious waste in the system, such as:

- Departments waiting for materials/information before they can proceed.
- Materials/information transported longer distances than necessary and stored to await the next step in the process.
- Unnecessary steps.
- Finished goods or services that must be stored because they're not needed yet.
- Excessive inventories anywhere in the stream.

You can create a current state value stream map for your organization by documenting the primary steps you take to transform raw materials and information into finished goods and services. One way to do this is to attach yourself to the material or information to be processed and record all that happens to it until it is delivered. When we do this for a client, we frequently start at the end. Anand learned this approach by working closely with Yoshiki Iwata, a member of the team that created the Toyota Production System. Iwata typically walked through a plant backward, beginning with shipping and moving upstream through each process. In this way, he could view each operation and process independently.

We use this method to spot opportunities, assess readiness, and identify barriers to change. We draw the map on a whiteboard so we can change it easily and when we've gone as far as the management team can go, we send team members out to gather critical information about the processes we've outlined.

The next step in the assessment process is to schedule interviews with key executives and managers throughout the organization. We spend about an hour with each person to understand his or her part of the business and identify strengths and weaknesses.

We talk about initial impressions, opportunities, an improvement approach, and the potential results the company could realize by taking this approach.

We finalize the current state value stream map, which we recreate electronically for further discussion. One part of the discussion is an estimate of value-added time as a percent of the total time from receipt of raw materials/information to delivery of finished goods and services. Value-added means transforming materials and information into products and services the customer wants. Non-value-added means consuming resources without directly contributing to the product or service. When we work with clients the first time, we often find that only about *2 percent* of the work being done is value added.

We spend some time teaching basic lean principles to the management team to prepare them for planning the next steps. We then engage team members in another value stream mapping exercise to create a future state map, which provides a hypothetical illustration of what the flow might look like if the most obvious waste was eliminated. The exercise helps create and cement a vision of how the leaders want to transform their business.

The vision leads to discussions of cultural change and what it takes to be successful. We identify the kaizen breakthrough events that need to be lined up to make this future state a reality, with most of the focus on the first event, as described in Chapter 2.

Late in the week, we reconvene to deliver our assessment feedback to the management team.

Planning the Transformation

Ray Stone came to Special Metals Wiggin in October 2003 just as the company came out of bankruptcy. Using his "kaizen eyes," he saw a tremendous amount of working capital tied up in inventory. He knew that reducing inventory freed up cash, which was important to a company emerging from bankruptcy.

An Operational Excellence Assessment along with the current and future state value stream maps revealed that lead time for two important products could be cut from sixteen weeks to ten days. Stone doubled that figure and offered a four-week lead time on those products to key customers. Within twelve months, kaizen breakthrough events, training, and continuous improvement activities had reduced inventory by 24 percent and doubled profitability, despite the high cost of raw materials.

As we noted in the previous chapter, the first dose of the antidote involves getting your house in order. We use three specific steps to plan the first phase, all of which draw on the assessment and value stream maps for direction.

STEP 1: THE GO FORWARD PLAN FOR PHYSICAL TRANSFORMATION

The Go Forward Plan identifies the actions during the first six months that will launch the transformation. Typical activities include extensive communication to increases awareness of the current situation, the compelling reasons to change, and a methodology for change that includes kaizen breakthrough events and training. The first kaizen breakthrough event, identified through the assessment and value stream maps, promises major impact in a short time. We want people to see the value and power of rapidly stripping out waste in a key process. Subsequent kaizen breakthrough events are operational in nature and narrow the focus to significant bottlenecks, specific quality issues, or problems uncovered during a kaizen event. Training targets leaders, managers, and supervisors to lay the groundwork for deploying and sustaining the transformation. The Managing for Daily Improvement training that middle managers and supervisors receive sharpens their knowledge and helps them learn how to sustain results.

Our Go Forward Plans list the information shown in the following example:

Date	Area	Activity	Target	Leader	Improvement	Remarks
June	Assembly line 1	First kaizen event	- 30% productivity improvement - 50% space reduction	VP Operations	$456,000	
July	Stamping area	Press set-up reduction	- 70% reduction	Department manager	$26,400	
Aug.	All supervisors	Managing for Daily Improvement	- Train all supervisors	VP HR	N/A	

Table 3-2 An Example of a Go Forward Plan

STEP 2: THE PLAN FOR CULTURAL TRANSFORMATION

The Cultural Transformation Plan prescribes training and other learning opportunities that will help change agents understand, lead, and sustain the transformation. Change agents are senior leaders and others who drive the process, including continuous improvement (CI) managers and facilitators. Exposing them to kaizen events outside the organization and to

Senior Management	1. Quest for the Perfect Engine workshop 2. Kaizen breakthrough workshop 3. TBM Executive Exchange

Corporate CI Manager	1. KPO Exchange
	2. Outside kaizen events
	  • Public
	  • Other clients
	3. KPO workshop

CI Facilitators	1. Outside kaizen events
	  • Public
	  • Other clients
	2. LeanSigma Black Belt training
	3. Kaizen instructor training

Finance/Accounting Managers	1. Lean Management Accounting workshop

Table 3-3   An Example of a Cultural Transformation Plan

training in the key concepts that support the transformation will help ensure its success.

Our Cultural Transformation Plans identify what training is needed by people in key positions, as the following example shows:

The first phase in the transformation from old management system to new is the entry phase, during which you get your house in order. Two things must happen during this phase to achieve operational excellence and prepare for growth:

1. You need to aggressively root out waste in critical areas of your value stream.
2. You need to get the right people in the right positions.

The assessment, value stream maps, and plans zero in on waste in key processes. At the same time, you need to minimize the waste that occurs when people's knowledge and skills are being underutilized.

STEP 3: GETTING THE RIGHT PEOPLE IN THE RIGHT PLACES

A key characteristic of a growth company is having each person perform competitively in his or her job. This is much broader than the ability to show up on time and do repetitive tasks well. Performing competitively means drawing on all the knowledge and skills employees can contribute by having them in the right jobs with the right training, tools, and direction, and the understanding that they share responsibility for the company's success. Leaders create the environment. Employees make it work.

Fred Heldenfels IV is president and CEO of Heldenfels Enterprises, which makes and installs precast concrete structures for buildings such as Astros Field, home of the Houston Astros baseball team, and SBC Center, home of the San Antonio Spurs basketball team. The company embarked on its lean journey in the fall of 2002. "The cultural change is leveraging responsibility further down in the organization so that supervisors and managers are the first line of responsibility for safety, cost, and customer satisfaction," said Fred. "There are more people out in the plant now who no longer have the attitude that this is just the way it is, and are instead asking why things are this way, and what can we do to change them. We've been able to harness that."

Fred's observation illustrates the most striking contrast between the scientific and transformational management systems: the role of employees. Frederick Taylor's scientific approach equated people with machines and sought the most efficient way to engage their hands in assembly line tasks. The new system is people-centric: It seeks to engage people's minds and involve them in using creativity to release the untapped potential of the organization.

Most people in most companies will resist this change. It's not that they don't welcome the chance to get involved in improving their processes, but few feel prepared to contribute, and nearly all expect the new system to quickly join the scrap pile of trendy programs that were also, at one time, the "latest and greatest." They are skeptics for good reason.

The success of the cultural transformation hinges on transforming a majority of skeptics into believers. In our experience, participation in kaizen events instills that belief. Paul Adelberg is the kaizen champion at Hayward Pool Products. He has people knocking on his door every day to propose a kaizen event. "The first thing that comes to mind when they have something they want to improve is to have a kaizen event," said Paul. "The reason is, we've never had a kaizen event where we didn't achieve or exceed our goals. We accomplish in one week what would typically take months to achieve. What has happened is that everyone eats, sleeps, and drinks kaizen." Nearly two-thirds of Hayward's hourly workers have participated in kaizen events, some in as many as twenty. "They're so passionate they want to do this all the time," Paul said.

Of course, participating in kaizen events alone will not transform a culture that has traditionally treated employees as commodities. A company must invest in people to fully realize their potential. People are the only appreciating asset a company has, yet we've been in board meetings where leaders have plunked down $40 million on an Enterprise Resource Planning (ERP) program while arguing against putting $40,000 into training. Employees must have the tools and training to effectively contribute, and that requires a commitment by leadership to fund it.

But that is still not enough. Even if most of your people are motivated, empowered, and trained, they must still be in the right positions to serve themselves and the organization well. Unlike the old management system, the new model relies on the right people being in the right places. If this isn't the case (and it never is when you start this journey), senior management must identify the misplaced and move or remove them.

We use a tool called Personalysis, developed by a Houston company of the same name, to understand the motivational needs of leaders and other change agents, get them in the ideal jobs, and build strong and complementary teams. Individuals complete a questionnaire that is analyzed to determine how they feel, think, and act under different levels of pressure. The Personalysis dimensions are:

- Rational: Preferred behavior; what you like to do.
- Socialized: Learned behavior for cooperating with others; what you ought to do.
- Instinctive: Safety and security needs; what you need to do.

The analysis reveals each person's personality and most likely behavior when working and interacting with others. Leaders use the profiles to help them determine which people belong in which positions and what mix of people would be best in different situations.

In some cases, you may find people who have been promoted beyond their capabilities. They need to be reassigned to positions in which they can become productive again. The adjustment will be difficult to make, but they will ultimately be happier and more effective—and so will the people around them.

Every organization with much of a history also has heroes who did great things in the distant past and then retired but didn't tell anyone. They've become deadweight that hard-working employees carry on their shoulders. You need to shake them from their lethargy or remove them, or the people carrying them will protest and productivity will suffer.

At the same time, you must reassure employees that no one will be laid off as a result of the transformation. They may be removed because they are not performing to the expectations of the job. They may be removed because they cannot deal with change. But they won't be laid off because their jobs disappear when processes become leaner.

"Pella has a longstanding practice of retaining our workforce," said president and CEO Mel Haught. "We reiterated that we would not have people lose jobs as a result of productivity improvements. People could change jobs, but they wouldn't lose their jobs.

"We were messing with people's jobs and lives and clearly they were skeptical, questioning whether this made sense," Mel said. "Change is always hard. Over time people have learned to expect change and that it's often for the better. It caught momentum and became self-sustaining."

Jason Incorporated, a diversified manufacturing company, just started its lean journey earlier this year. Headquartered in Milwaukee with four operations throughout the U.S. and thirteen foreign countries, the company wanted to accelerate growth that had been relatively flat for five years. In the first year of the journey, president and CEO David Westgate has already replaced three division presidents. "About six months into the process, you find out who's really committed and who isn't," he said. "It's imperative that senior management is 100 percent behind this. We had three guys saying the right things, but not doing the right things."

Like Pella, Jason Incorporated has committed to not laying people off because of improvements in productivity. When it frees up space through kaizen events—it will do 130 events in its first year—it ropes off the empty area and puts up a sign: *Reserved for New Business.* "We want to use lean as a growth strategy," said David.

The early results from kaizen events and other actions convince most employees that the transformation—the antidote for the dis-ease they feel—is necessary and positive. Most, but not all. Even positive changes generate resistance. We call these hold-outs "anchor draggers" or "cave" people: citizens against virtually everything. We recommend dealing with the anchor draggers through two approaches.

First, change management's focus from the negative to the positive, as shown by the "wedges" in the bottom of Figure 3-1. Involve the change agents, your organization's "movers and shakers," in early kaizen events. Applaud their contributions. Place them on the fast track to promotions into positions where they can more directly influence change. Send a fre-

Figure 3-1 Managing Resistance

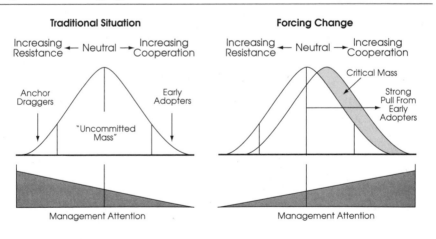

quent, consistent message to all employees that the transformation is permanent and those who support it are rising stars.

As for the anchor draggers, invest as little energy in them as possible. In our experience, what often happens is their peers eventually deselect them and ask to have them moved out or fired. If they still choose not to support the organization's new direction, you will have to deal with them like a cancer to be removed.

Or absorbed. "When we looked at our people, at who were vocal and negative, they were the first people we got on kaizen teams," said Barb King, who runs Landscape Structures with her husband, Steve. "We put them on my team and on Steve's team and on the VP of Operations' team so they could work through it and everyone was converted."

People aren't the most important asset an organization has; good people are. Put them in the right positions, arm them with the training and tools they need, point them in the right direction, and your culture *will* change.

That starts with leadership.

CHAPTER FOUR

Leading the Transformation

Leadership is all about creating and sustaining a superior value proposition. A value proposition is the tangible benefit your target markets receive from your products or services. Superior value propositions deliver superior results for your customers, including innovative designs, additional services, lower costs, quicker response and faster time to market, and higher satisfaction.

A superior value proposition sets your company up for long-term growth and success. It puts ever-increasing distance between you and your competitors. It aligns all activities and improves efficiency through a singular focus. It boosts market share and locks in customers. It provides value nobody else can match.

You create and sustain a superior value proposition in four ways:

- *Operational effectiveness:* You are the most productive and effective organization winning the race against competitors.
- *Value innovation:* You are closest to the customers' real needs.

- *Differentiation*: You offer the most valuable products and services.
- *New value proposition*: You change the rules to run a different race.

Operational effectiveness must come first. It is the first phase in the journey from old management system to new, the entry phase during which you get your house in order. It requires assimilating and implementing the very best lean practices in your value chain to compete effectively. It demands speed in execution to stay ahead of the competition.

Through operational excellence, you run the same race faster. At some point, you are so far ahead of your competitors that they will never catch up. The reason Toyota and other industry leaders willingly share their best practices with competitors is to continually improve and avoid complacency, and because they know their competitors cannot catch them. It took Toyota decades to develop a culture and management system that focus daily on improving quality and speed. Competitors can learn from that system. They can assimilate and implement Toyota's best practices, but they cannot duplicate its culture. As they improve, it motivates Toyota's employees to improve even more, thus maintaining their lead through operational excellence.

Yet operational excellence alone will not suffice forever. The strongest competitors who achieve high levels of performance will realize that they cannot win this race forever and they must choose to run a different race. This choice is available to any company, whether leader or follower, in any industry.

You choose to run a different race by strategic positioning, which involves plotting an integrated strategy that provides a unique, long-term advantage in your chosen space. The new value proposition must create sustainable long-term growth in economic value as measured by return on invested capital (ROIC).

You use strategic positioning derived from value innovation, differentiation, and a new value proposition to make your company unique because being unique creates wealth and long-term growth. For example, Dell's innovative approach to selling computer hardware directly to its customers bypasses the distribution networks of its competitors, allowing Dell to customize machines and deliver them quickly at a reasonable price. The approach is only possible because of Dell's operational efficiency. It partners with key suppliers to have material delivered to its manufacturing facilities as needed. No more than eight hours of inventory exist in its factories and no more than seventy-two hours exist across the entire organization. Dell's supplied parts come from trucks backed up to the plant for that day's production. Dell turns its inventory 107 times a year, compared to 8.5 for Hewlett-Packard, which many experts believe could translate into an advantage of eight margin points. When you consider that HP's net margin on PCs may hover around one percent, Dell has a dominant competitive advantage.

Computers are "pulled" through Dell's manufacturing process to fill customer orders, not pushed for storage in retailers' warehouses. No computer is built without an order, and most are built to order in four to eight hours—more than 80,000 computers every twenty-four hours.

Dell's value stream produces less waste than its competitors. Its inventory of raw materials and finished goods is low. It integrates new technology more quickly. Dealing directly with customers puts it in a better position to identify and respond to their needs. It controls price by eliminating the extra expense incurred by distributors.

Rather than compete with IBM, Hewlett-Packard, and Compaq on their terms, Michael Dell chose to run a different race. In 1984, few took him seriously when he said he would take on industry leader IBM. Dell passed IBM in global market share in 1999. In the last ten years, Dell's U.S. market share has jumped from 5 percent to 33 percent. It has become the global leader with a 17.9 percent share worldwide in 2004, nearly two percentage points higher than second place Hewlett-Packard.

IBM's global market share in 2004 was 5.9 percent.

Dell illustrates the power of an effective value proposition executed with speed through integrated activities in a tailored value chain. It also illustrates the necessity of sticking to your vision. The few times Dell has faltered in the past twenty years was because it strayed from its chosen path, such as when it briefly tried selling computers indirectly through warehouse clubs and computer superstores in 1991. A great strategy requires focusing on the "vital few" that promise the best chance of growth and success. Trade-offs must be made. Deciding what *not* to do is even more important than deciding what to pursue.

Every industry holds the potential for someone to run a different race, to redefine the rules so dramatically that competitors must scramble to survive or abandon the race. To explore that potential in your industry, consider the following questions:

- Do you start with what is and feel overpowered by constraints, or what could be and dream of possibilities?
- Do you take industry conditions as a given and let that frame your idea of what is possible, or do you challenge their seemingly inevitable nature and conventional wisdom to expose new opportunities?
- Do you focus on outpacing the competition in every aspect, or on developing a radically new and superior value curve that will let you dominate the market?
- Do you focus on segmenting and retaining existing customers, or do you search for deeper, unarticulated customer needs that unlock a new mass of buyers—even if that means willingly letting some existing customers go?

Leadership is all about creating and sustaining a superior value proposition. How you do that, how you systematically improve organizational effectiveness while pursuing strategic opportunities, how you excel at the race you're in while preparing for a different race, how you decide what to pursue and what to ignore and what to deselect, and how you move the organization as one toward your strategic direction is the subject of this chapter.

It's a process. It can be learned. It can produce a superior value proposition. And it can focus your entire company on generating long-term growth.

LEADERSHIP AT VERMEER

Gary Vermeer was an inventor. One of his first inventions was a modified farm wagon with a mechanical hoist that created such a demand that Gary started the Vermeer Manufacturing Company in Pella, Iowa, in 1948.

Early on, the company brought innovation to the agricultural industry, introducing the world's first large, round hay baler and a number of other machines that transformed modern hay production. Vermeer also applied its expertise to other fields, entering the construction, environmental, and industrial equipment industries. In 1991, it rolled out a horizontal directional drilling machine for installing fiber optic cable. Its trenching equipment is used on road construction and mining projects. It manufactures chippers, grinders, and stump cutters for a variety of landscaping jobs. It makes compact excavators and terrain levelers.

By the mid-1990s, the company, now more than 2,000 strong, had outgrown its facilities. Sales continued to rise, but profits had declined, and a lot of capital was tied up in inventory. On the advice of an outside board member, the company looked into lean. After two years of study, Vermeer embarked on its lean journey.

Its first kaizen events involved production people in rearranging equipment to improve flow. "We thought we had people on board," said Mary Andringa, president and CEO, "but then we'd come back the next day and it was all back the way it was before."

The antidote started to take hold when all senior executives participated in kaizen breakthrough events. The minimum requirement was three to six events in the first year. Mary was on twelve events in the first twenty-four months. "We had some pushback," she said. An economic downturn from 2001 to 2003 shrunk the management team, leaving leaders who were committed to the journey. The average number of events for each of the nine members of Vermeer's executive team is nineteen. Mary has participated in twenty-nine. Seventy percent of employees have been on at least one event, and those who have participated average eight events per employee. Participation would be higher, but Vermeer has added about 500 new people to its ranks.

Employee participation extends beyond kaizen breakthrough events. Through its *Expect the Best* process, employees submit ideas aligned with the company's lean metrics for quality, delivery, safety, and cost. In a recent twenty-four-month span, Vermeer implemented more than 10,000 ideas.

Vermeer prioritizes and aligns these efforts through lean and policy deployment. Policy deployment is a process for focusing a company's resources on those few critical objectives that improve execution and drive growth. As shown in Figure 4-1, policy deployment is an integral part of the senior management leadership process that lies at the center of an organization's transformation.

WHY TRANSFORMATIONS FAIL

Dr. Ryuji Fukuda, an independent consultant from Japan, has devoted more than fifty years to the study of management. One of the few individuals to win the Deming Prize for his contributions to productivity and quality improvement, Dr. Fukuda has helped a number of companies transform their management systems, including Sony, Nikon, Timken, Ferrari, Pratt & Whitney, Volvo, and Michelin.

In Dr. Fukuda's experience, lean transformations fail because of a lack of management direction, a lack of time (too much to do), a lack of resources, and/or a lack of cooperation with other departments. To eliminate these weaknesses, he developed an x-type matrix that organizations can use to define business objectives, select key projects, set goals, establish implementation teams, and align all units, divisions, departments, teams, and individuals. The matrix enhanced a planning process called hoshin kanri, first used in 1965 by Komatsu to set that company's direction. The more popular term for the process today is *policy deployment*.

For TBM, the genesis of its policy deployment process was in 1987 when Anand, who was working for American Standard at the time, met with an executive of Hoxan JV in Tokyo. The executive, who had studied both U.S. and Japanese companies, pointed out that they looked very similar at 30,000 feet, but that one difference stood out upon closer

Figure 4-1   Senior Leadership Management Process

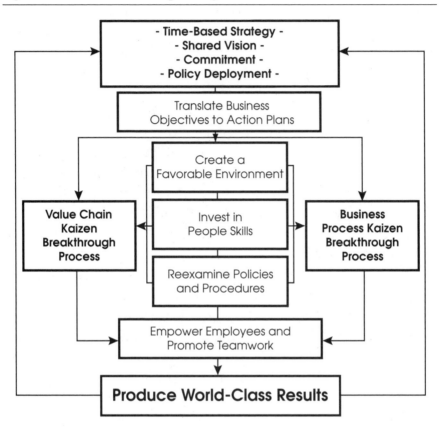

scrutiny: American leaders make executive decisions faster while Japanese leaders execute better.

Policy deployment is a way to make better decisions faster. It accelerates the planning process through proven tools for collecting and analyzing information, identifying objectives, and selecting projects. Most of us are familiar with strategic planning marathons that take six months to crank out a pound of plans. The policy deployment process we will describe takes about two weeks and produces a plan summarized on a single page: the x-type matrix created by Dr. Fukuda.

Ultimately, the four reasons Dr. Fukuda gave for failed transformations end up on senior management's doorstep. As we mentioned earlier, this revolution is brought about by leaders, not by discontented masses. If senior leaders lack a vision, it will fail. If they delegate the leadership of it, it will fail. If they don't fund it, it will fail. If they allow business units, divisions, and departments to set their own priorities, it will fail. But if they are committed to the transformation and if that commitment is tangible through personal involvement and necessary resources and consistent communication, it will succeed. And that success will produce world-class results as we've seen already at Hayward Pool Products, Landscape Structures, Western Union, WIKA USA, Deli Express, Iowa DNR, Pella, Ventana, Hubbell, Toyota, Dell, and others.

HOW LEAN LEADERS ACT

In our experience, the most effective leaders immerse themselves in the transformation. They spend more time talking to customers and employees than sitting in their offices. They care more about studying their organization's value stream than studying its stock performance. Each day they display their personal commitment to and involvement in the activities that will create and sustain growth. They prefer action over theory. They lead by example, not by sending memos.

Perhaps most importantly, they are passionate about what their organizations do. We would guess that 70 to 80 percent of today's leaders have no passion for what they sell, and yet, when you look at the leaders of some of our greatest companies, the one attribute they share is a passion for their businesses. Look at Bill Gates or Michael Dell, Herb Kelleher at Southwest Airlines, Jeff Bezos at Amazon.com, Charles Schwab, and Starbucks' Howard Schultz, to name a few. It's one of the reasons Toyota doesn't hunt for outside presidents and CEOs to lead the company: They haven't lived Toyota and cannot understand—or feel passionate about—its culture.

WIKA's Michael Gerster summed up the problem when he observed that American and European managers "want to work less *in* the business and more *for* the business. The leader has to write the script about what differentiates the company from other contenders in a crowded marketplace," he said, "and you won't be able to write it unless you understand your customers' perceptions of value and how your company can bridge the gap between reality and expectations through continuous improvement." If you're passionate about what your company does, you won't be happy unless you're working *in* the business, and that means learning customer needs, understanding your company's capabilities, and leading the daily effort to bridge the gap.

Leadership requires vision, customer-focus, communication, innovation, alignment, measurement, discipline, and continuous improvement. Based on our work with hundreds of lean leaders, we have identified twelve actions required of leaders to initiate and sustain a cultural transformation. As you read through the list, think about the activities that currently occupy your work days and how they would have to change to accommodate these twelve actions, for not only must transformation extend to leadership, it must start there.

Twelve Actions of Lean Leaders

1. ***Create a sense of urgency.*** With a growing global marketplace and increasingly aggressive competition, no company needs to create the urgency for change. It is already there. Most leaders understand this. Your job is to make sure your employees understand it, too.

2. ***Change the focus.*** Shift attention away from the past and toward the future, beginning with turning from an analysis of past customer interactions, to personal insights into the solutions your customers need now and will need going forward.

3. ***Develop leaders.*** Find, groom, and motivate the leaders you need to transform your organization, and then put them in the right positions to drive the change.

4. ***Communicate openly and often.*** You exhibit your commitment to the transformation through such actions as visiting customers,

participating in kaizen events, and communicating key elements of the transformation relentlessly, in existing and new forums, with all employees, over and over and over again.

5. *Focus on your customers.* We recommend that all senior leaders spend at least one week a month with key customers. We will offer ideas on what to do during that week in the next chapter. You need to be among the collectors of customer information that can be used to develop innovative solutions.

6. *Encourage and sustain innovation.* Kaizen events help participants experience rapid innovation. Idea programs like the one in place at Vermeer encourage innovative thinking by all employees. You must teach the organization to recognize unconventional opportunities that can help you lock up your customers.

7. *Align through policy deployment.* No organization can afford to waste energy and resources on efforts that do not support its objectives. You can use policy deployment to build consensus on a few, critical things that will generate growth and long-term success.

8. *Allocate resources to ensure success.* You are likely to spend less on equipment, facilities, and technology, and more on people, processes, and projects that support your business objectives.

9. *Measure progress.* You need to identify metrics that capture the implications of your strategy on multiple levels, collect and analyze the data, and develop countermeasures when goals are not reached.

10. *Extend the transformation across your value chain.* Once you've achieved a level of operational excellence, the second phase of the transformation involves suppliers, distributors and customers in effective planning and the seamless delivery of value.

11. *Promote continuous improvement.* The notion that every task and every process can be improved—no matter how often they have already been improved—is one characteristic of the transformational management system. Leaders must applaud the improvements of today while demanding further improvements tomorrow.

12. *Maintain discipline and focus*. As the initial buzz wears off, people naturally slip back into old habits. Sustaining the transformation is a challenge for every organization. You will need to conduct regular reviews—daily, weekly, and monthly—of organizational performance and hold people accountable to keep the transformation on track.

Throughout this book, we present proven approaches for taking many of the actions on this list. None will be effective without the personal, visible, and passionate commitment of senior leaders to revitalizing their organizations. In his book, *The Toyota Way*, Jeffrey K. Liker poses three questions you can ask to determine if the minimum level of leadership commitment exists to begin the transformation:

- Are top executives who run the company committed to a long-term vision of adding value to customers and society in general?
- Are top executives who run the company committed to developing and involving employees and partners?
- Will there be continuity in top leadership's philosophy?

As Liker suggests, if the answer to any of these questions is "no," the organization should postpone the transformation and focus instead on short-term improvement.

If, however, the answers are "yes," leaders should express their commitment by embracing the actions listed above. But commitment is only the first step. Employees need to know what you—and they—are committing to. They need to know what your direction for the company—its mission and vision—means in their day-to-day activities.

This is a challenge for companies that have taken the time to create a mission and vision, post them throughout their facilities, talk about them at employee meetings—and then pretty much ignore them. Some even try to link their strategic plans with their mission and vision, but the connection is often forced and quickly forgotten in the "busy-ness" of business. Employees know what's important: It's what they're told to work on *today*. If what they're told to work on has no visible connection to their organization's mission and vision, the direction chosen by leaders and captured in the mission and vision will not be followed.

Leaders need a process for translating mission and vision into objectives and plans that employees must act upon for the company to succeed. That process is called *policy deployment*. Through policy deployment, senior leadership's commitment to transforming the organization becomes tangible in the action plans they approve and own. The action plans focus everyone in the organization on those vital few areas that must be addressed to make progress on the mission and vision. In this way, policy deployment enables leaders to act on their commitment and execute their vision.

FOCUSING ON THE VITAL FEW

The transformational management system treats strategic planning much the same way it treats leadership, employees, customers, suppliers, and processes, which is to say very differently than the old system. Policy deployment takes significantly less time than the old approach to strategic planning. It gives everyone involved in the process equal input into the outcomes. It ensures that the necessary buy-in and resources exist before the plan is implemented. It demands relentless accountability and follow-up to achieve objectives. It delivers results aligned with the organization's vision, its need for operational excellence, and its desire for growth.

"We do a top-down, bottom-up process," said Tim Powers, president and CEO at Hubbell. Hubbell engineers, manufactures, and sells electrical and electronic products such as wiring systems and lighting for offices, products for the utility infrastructure, and specialty communication products. It employs more than 11,000 people with annual sales of $2 billion. "The major benefit is that management as a team reassesses where it is on an annual basis. It helps us focus on the vital few and get rid of the typical problems facing most companies of having too many priorities."

Tim and his leadership team embarked on their lean journey late in 2001. "We were in a situation where we had too much working capital, our ability to adapt to rapidly changing market conditions was too slow, and we needed to be quicker, more flexible, more able," said Tim. "I thought our company needed dramatic change."

In 2002, the first full year of its lean journey, Hubbell coined a "2x4" strategy: two times improvement by 2004. Its goals included 2x inventory turns by '04, 2 margin points by '04, and 2 percentage point market share improvement by '04. The "2x4" strategy helped the organization focus on the vital few goals that would help Hubbell improve speed, flexibility, and quality. It started in six sites and expanded to all thirty of its locations by 2004, a steady transition that makes its results even more astounding. From 2001 to 2004, Hubbell made dramatic improvements including:

- Net sales up 54 percent
- Net income up 320 percent
- Sales per employee up 17 percent
- Inventory down 53 percent and inventory turns doubled
- Working capital as a percent of sales down 45 percent
- Space reduction of more than 1.5 million square feet

"Our new management methodology has helped us take several hundred million dollars out of working capital and put it into cash," said Tim, "and that's allowed us to buy more companies." Hubbell's acquisition strategy is a key component of its plans to grow the company. It has used policy deployment since 2002 to select—and deselect—the objectives and actions that support its strategies.

HOW POLICY DEPLOYMENT WORKS

As Figure 4-1 shows, the senior management leadership process begins with strategy, vision, commitment, and policy deployment. Policy deployment begins with knowledge of the facts. The initial policy deployment meeting takes three days, typically off-site, and must be attended by the entire management team and other key contributors.

STEP 1: CREATE A COMMON UNDERSTANDING

We believe that everyone involved in identifying strategies and developing plans should share the same information. They should have a common understanding of the external environment (opportunities and threats) and internal environment (strengths and weaknesses), short- and long-term goals, and strategic direction, so that they can provide informed and reasoned insights.

We don't subscribe to the idea that participants in this process should be limited to the president/CEO and his or her direct reports. Every organization has additional "movers and shakers" and informal leaders who can enrich the discussions and strengthen the plan. We encourage you to find the natural "go-to" people who have their coworkers' confidence and respect and tactfully bring them into the process. The ideal number of participants seems to be between twelve and twenty, although we've done policy deployment with fewer and larger groups.

Before the first meeting, determine who will present the critical information to the group that it needs to make decisions. Topics to be addressed include:

- Customers' perceptions of quality, delivery, service, and value (each key customer/market segment)
- Competitors' strengths and weaknesses
- Current company performance
- Impediments to success
- Operational performance indicators
- Financial performance indicators
- Human resource capabilities and challenges
- Supplier capabilities and challenges
- Economic, legal, regulatory, environmental, and other issues
- Emerging technology and its implied impact on the organization's future

The presentations and discussions during the first meeting should be completed in approximately three hours. It's important early in this meeting to clearly communicate the egalitarian nature of this process. We say "one person, one vote." All ranks and titles are left at the door. Participants need to understand this because each has an equal responsibility for the creation and success of the plan.

STEP 2: ANALYZE STRENGTHS, WEAKNESSES, OPPORTUNITIES, AND THREATS (SWOT)

The information gathered during the first meeting is used for the focused SWOT analysis in the second part of the meeting. The goal of the SWOT analysis is to identify those significant, vital few issues the organization must address.

Strengths and weaknesses are generally assessed from an internal focus and against customer expectations and competitive pressures.

Opportunities and threats are assessed from an external perspective and are generally out of your control.

The exercise begins by asking participants to assume that each is the president or leading executive of the company. If they were the boss, what would their priorities be?

Each person writes down three strengths, one each on a Post-It note. Each strength should be a clear, concise, and complete statement. The participant then prioritizes the strengths by putting stars in the upper right-hand corner: *** for the top priority, ** for number two, and * for number three. The participant repeats the process for the weaknesses, and then prints his or her name on the bottom right-hand corner of each note. Participants are encouraged to take their time, but not to discuss their ideas with others in the group. The goal of this silent brainstorming activity is get everyone involved: One person, one vote.

Once this is completed, participants follow the same process for key opportunities and threats. When everyone is finished, the facilitators take their notes and arrange them on a wall by strengths, weaknesses, opportunities, and threats, and under similar categories or sentiments within each. All participants have a chance to review the groupings to make sure their ideas are understood and categorized correctly.

When the review is complete, beginning with strengths, the number of stars under each category is counted to select the top three or four areas for synthesis. Each area is assigned to a sub-team charged with capturing the intent and spirit of all related ideas in a single, concise, clear statement and presenting its statement to the entire group for further synthesis, improvement, and a reality check. Once the group agrees on the nature and wording of the selected strengths, it repeats the process for weaknesses, opportunities, and threats.

Table 4-1 shows what one of our clients produced through this exercise.

STEP 3: DEVELOP DIRECTIONAL ALIGNMENT

Leadership's most important step is to align the direction of their organization with the company's vision and the revelations of the SWOT analysis. Leaders determine this direction by evaluating two dimensions, technology/products and markets/channels, to expose both new and related opportunities.

The directional alignment exercise typically involves the same group that participated in the SWOT analysis. It begins with the group suggesting new and related products the company could offer, new and related technologies it could pursue, new and related markets it could enter, and new and related channels it could explore. Sub-teams of the group define each new/related opportunity and anticipate its potential, impact, capital required, and risk. They present their conclusions to the entire group, which then uses the same silent brainstorming technique described in Step 2 to select the top five high potential/high impact areas with low capital/low risk rating.

Sub-teams for each of the top five areas identify their area's impact on sales and earnings, and its capital and other resource requirements. They outline the action steps and implementation schedule necessary to move forward. They then describe their findings to the entire group,

Strengths
- Financial strength and stability enables growth plans.
- Ability to leverage longstanding portfolio of strong brand names.
- Strong, disciplined leadership team focused on a well-defined vision.

Weaknesses
- Lack of management depth and breadth limits our ability to more rapidly execute strategic initiatives.
- Current operational performance limits our ability to create a competitive service advantage and improve ROIC.
- Lack of adequate scale to take advantage of internal operational and external market opportunities

Opportunities
- Positioned to take advantage of targeted acquisition opportunities.
- Gain market share from Competitor X through differentiation by consistently superior service performance.
- Increase participation in available markets through major product expansion.

Threats
- Consolidation of competitors and channel partners.
- Low-cost foreign manufacturers directly serving the North American market.
- Continual decline of North American industrial markets.

Table 4-1   Example of Focused SWOT Analysis

which discusses the plans, completes the strategic directional matrix, and reviews each plan and all plans together for practicality.

STEP 4: OUTLINE THE STRATEGIC PLAN—POLICY DEPLOYMENT PHASE I

Policy deployment is a three-phase process that begins with the development of goals that are then translated into objectives and projects through the policy deployment matrix, which are reviewed monthly throughout the year to ensure that the objectives are being met.

The SWOT analysis and strategic directional matrix are key inputs for Phase I. The planning team uses these inputs to outline a three- to

Figure 4-2   Strategic Directional Matrix

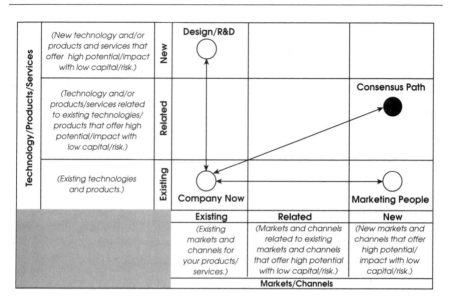

five-year strategic plan that identifies concrete and quantitative goals in four specific areas:

- Quality/customer satisfaction
- Productivity/cost reduction
- Delivery/responsiveness
- Morale/ergonomics/safety

Once the goals are established, the team reviews current performance on them and establishes concrete, measurable goals for each operating unit that will contribute to achieving the overall business goals.

STEP 5: CREATE THE MATRIX—POLICY DEPLOYMENT PHASE II

The policy deployment matrix captures business objectives, projects, goals, financial impact, and implementation teams for the organization or for individual business units on a single page, as shown in Figure 4-3.

Figure 4-3   Policy Deployment Matrix Example

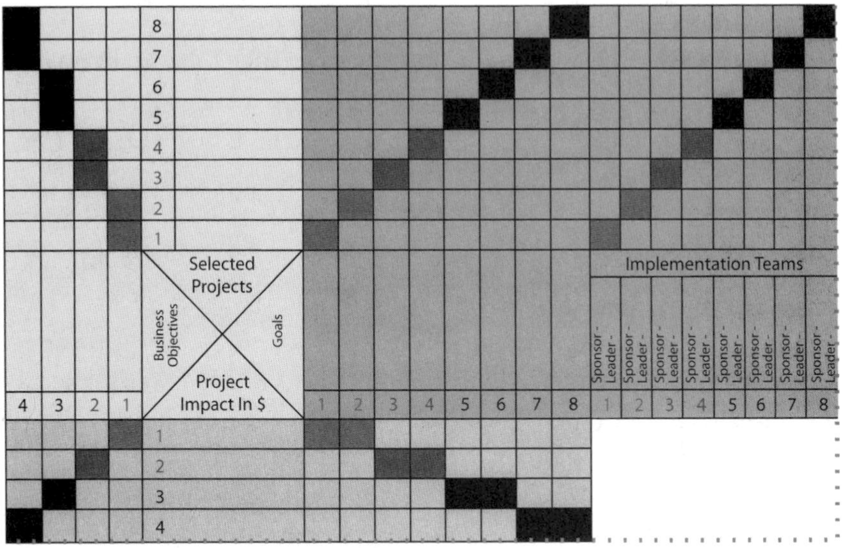

To complete the matrix, the leadership team for the organization or business unit groups the strengths and opportunities identified during the SWOT analysis to guide the development of growth objectives. It then groups the weaknesses and threats to help develop operational improvement objectives. We refer to growth objectives as "offensive" and operational improvement objectives as "defensive," or basic "blocking and tackling." In our experience, the focus of the first year of the transformation is on the defensive side, on shoring up the weaknesses and threats and getting your house in order. Through operational excellence, your organization earns the right to go on the offensive and plan for growth.

With both a defensive and offensive focus in mind, each member of the leadership team develops three prioritized business objectives that are broad enough to address specific SWOT statements (see Table 4-1), yet specific enough to produce achievable, measurable annual targets. As in Step 2, each participant writes down his or her three objectives on Post-It notes, using stars to prioritize them and printing his/her name on each. Again, the goal of this silent brainstorming activity is get everyone involved, although we notice that people tend to be "gun shy" the first time around.

When everyone is finished, the facilitators arrange their notes on a wall under similar areas of focus. All participants have a chance to review the groupings to make sure their ideas are understood and categorized correctly.

When the review is complete, the entire team uses the grouping and the stars to select the top three or four business objectives for the coming year. Each objective is assigned to a sub-team charged with capturing the intent and spirit of all related ideas in a single, clear, concise statement. The team then identifies one, two, or, at the most, three specific projects required to achieve the objective, key measures for success for each, and the potential financial impact of completing the projects and meeting the objective.

Each sub-team presents its business objective with project plans, metrics, and financial impact to the entire group for discussion and refinement. The leadership team must choose which projects to pursue with six being ideal and eight projects the maximum. When all objectives have been finalized, the objectives, projects, goals (metrics), and financial impact are entered on the policy deployment matrix, an example of which is shown in Figure 4-3. The different shades of gray show the alignment of these elements. The example has been condensed by eliminating projects three through seven.

The last section of the matrix involves identification of the implementation teams for each project, beginning with the project leader and, if this is for a business unit, a project sponsor at the corporate level. The project leader/sponsor must have been present for the policy deployment process and cannot lead or participate on more than two teams.

The leadership team then selects four to eight members for each project implementation team depending on the size and scope of the project. When we facilitate these activities, we screen people to make sure that the right people end up on the right teams. Implementation team members must represent different functions, bring the customer viewpoint to the project, and provide the necessary technical expertise. We look for a balance of passion and knowledge, process insiders and outsiders, executives and managers, and other cross-functional perspectives that help create innovative solutions while achieving the objectives.

As with the project sponsor/leader, an implementation team member cannot be on more than two teams.

"We establish a policy deployment matrix with our top managers," said Hubbell's Tim Powers, "then each business unit aligns its priorities with that. Every single unit ties to our policy deployment matrix. Our goals are the sum of the outcomes of our business units."

STEP 6: CHOOSE THE VITAL FEW AND DESELECT AGGRESSIVELY

The projects chosen through policy deployment are not the only activities people are working on. The purpose of this step is to select only the vital few breakthrough initiatives that will have a major impact on the company and deselect those that won't, because in addition to these initiatives, people are working on many important activities daily to maintain current levels and achieve superior performance.

We start by asking leadership team members to do a little homework: List all the breakthrough initiatives in which they are involved. Breakthrough initiatives focus on growth: (1) in sales and market share over and above maintaining the current business level; (2) in earnings and asset leverage over and above maintaining the current level of performance; and, (3) to achieve your mission through strategic alignment with long-range plans.

As a group, the participants put their initiatives in five categories:

- Regulatory, and you have to do them
- Mandatory, and your job depends on them (so you can't tactfully negotiate relief)
- Aligned with the policy deployment matrix
- Aligned strategically
- Not aligned

Deselection involves keeping those aligned strategically and by policy deployment and the regulatory initiatives, killing those not aligned, and questioning the mandatory to see if they must be kept. The group needs to formally "kill" each deselected project and develop action plans for questionable ones.

Deselecting can be a very tedious process because nobody wants to give anything up. But as Hubbell discovered, it is absolutely necessary. "It helps us focus on the vital few and get rid of the typical problem most companies have of facing too many priorities," said Tim Powers. "Deselection is vital for making progress as a corporation."

We encourage leadership teams to meet after two or three weeks to finalize the policy deployment matrix. This allows time for the ramifications of the matrix to become clear and for a "sanity check" to occur.

STEP 7: TRACK AND REVIEW PERFORMANCE— POLICY DEPLOYMENT PHASE III

As the name implies, the crux of policy deployment is making sure projects are on track and that actions are taken to achieve the business objectives. This is done through monthly project reviews by senior management.

As soon as the policy deployment matrix is complete, leaders develop a detailed monthly schedule for reviewing performance. Following a detailed tracking procedure, each month the executive team reviews the projects that have failed to achieve targeted milestones and devises and implements countermeasures. Visual controls and performance boards help everyone in the organization see how the company—and each team—is doing.

We will describe this step and communication of the plan in more detail in Chapter 8.

THE POWER OF ALIGNMENT

High-performing organizations accelerate improvements and speed past the competition through the power of alignment. If everyone is working on those activities that are vital to your growth and success, your company will grow and succeed, as Hubbell continues to demonstrate.

"The general and agreed upon priorities of our company are innovating the greatest number of products, and serving our markets with the least amount of capital," said Hubbell's Tim Powers. It aligns all business units with these priorities through a one-day policy deployment review process. "We have sixteen managers in our top management team. We start from scratch every year with a SWOT analysis: what has gone on, how we saw it a year ago, what's changed. We get the skeleton of the matrix that day and then take it out into the field and fill it out during discussions at our locations, to get the exact goals and measures. We do this in the fall so we're ready to go at the beginning of December."

This process takes place at a company with more than 150 different product lines that is reorganizing along those product lines to better serve its customers. The most effective alignment—of policy deployment, product/service development, functional activities, human resources, value streams, and other key processes—begins with the customer. The mission and vision of the organization, and the policy deployment matrix that translates that mission and vision, begin with the customer.

Most organizations assume they know what their customers need. Such assumptions keep them from gaining intimate knowledge of who their customers are and what they require. The first step to creating satisfied and loyal customers is to admit your ignorance of their real needs. The second step is to uncover those needs, to hear the "Voice of the Customer."

CHAPTER FIVE

Discovering the Voice of the Customer

We've had a lot of clients lately asking for help with lean who wanted to start right away with the growth side of the journey. We tell them "no," you have to start with operational excellence first. You need to improve quality, consistency, and reliability, and create capacity to grow organically and leverage your fixed assets and expenses. Once you get quality, delivery, and costs under control, once you've freed up time and space by eliminating non-value-added activities, you've earned the right to grow. Start too soon and your growth efforts will inevitably suffer and you will fail to create profit leverage.

The second phase of the lean transformation is *synchronization*, aligning your supply and demand chains to offer greater value to your customers than the competition. You can't begin the second phase until the first phase, *operational excellence*, has started creating capacity, which usually happens in the second year of the journey.

Gary worked with Huck Fastening Systems before coming to TBM. The company had two years of very flat demand in its aerospace market, during which it gained significant capacity by focusing on lean. When the aerospace floodgates opened in the late 1990s, the demand for fasteners increased nearly 100 percent in three years. Huck Fastening Systems filled that demand with the same equipment and people it had when the market turned around. Its high level of operational excellence positioned it for rapid growth through leverage, and its return on assets jumped from 10 percent to nearly 40 percent.

But Huck Fastening Systems wasn't content just to fill orders. It sent teams of people to its customers' sites to watch them work and observe what they needed. Fasteners account for nearly half of the parts used to build an airplane; in the case of a Boeing 767, for example, more than two million fasteners hold one airplane together.

The team learned that assemblers who build the wing panels on a 767, each of which is about sixty feet long, wasted time walking back and forth to get more fasteners. The solution? Every six feet along the wing, Huck Fastening Systems hung the right amount of fasteners for that section. The solution not only made the assemblers more efficient, but it also reduced the number of handlers Huck Fastening Systems had to provide and the amount of inventory it needed.

The team also noticed that the guns used to attach the fasteners wore out and that replacing them meant making assemblers wait. Huck Fastening Systems partnered with a local supplier to provide replacements within ten minutes and opened a tool repair section to extend the life of Boeing's tools. As a result of these and other innovative solutions, Huck Fastening Systems increased its share of Boeing's business, as well as the price of its fasteners, while making it harder for competitors to vie for Boeing's business.

As Huck Fastening Systems discovered, the lean journey frees up lots of capacity that can be used to grow the company. To grow, you need a new approach to observing, listening, and learning from your customers. You must be guided by the Voice of the Customer.

WHAT DOES YOUR COMPANY DO?

When people ask you what your company does, how do you typically respond? If the company is a manufacturer, the most common reply begins with, "We make stuff." If it's a service company, the answer is often the primary service you provide, as in, "We're an insurance company," or "We provide accounting services."

If someone asked your key customers what your company does, they would probably get similar answers: You supply specific materials or services that they need. You occupy a slot in their supply chain. You are important, but you are rarely irreplaceable because the materials or services you provide can be bought from your competitors.

The goal is to make your company irreplaceable, and that begins with a different answer to the question about what your company does. "The old system of 'we make stuff, you buy stuff' is over," said WIKA's Michael Gerster. "I believe a company's strength is determined by the level of customer dependence. I want to increase our customers' dependency on WIKA as a valuable partner."

If you think of your company in terms of the traditional products and services it provides—the "we make stuff, you buy stuff" mentality—you are seriously limiting your ability to grow by partnering with customers. A partnership implies a closer relationship in which each partner depends on the other for its success. Such a relationship requires a deeper understanding of what your customers' need.

We see evidence of inadequate processes for learning what customers' need in almost every company we study. Between 70 and 80 percent of new products or services fail to meet development cost and revenue expectations. New products and services buckle under the weight of rich feature sets because the company doesn't understand which features its customers truly value. Critical departments like sales, marketing, and engineering claim they know what customers want, but don't agree on what it is. Instead of developing innovative new products and services, companies reduce prices, introduce new advertising, expand their presence at trade shows, and quote shorter lead times. All of this is necessary because they don't know what their customers' really need.

In Vermeer's case, the company relied on dealers and its field people for customer input. "In the fall of 2003, we had a series of four or five focus group events with our dealers," said Kevin Alft, vice president of Underground Installation Solutions. "The dealers typically came up with incremental improvements: This competitor has this feature and we need it, too. So it was primarily playing catch-up. I was very dissatisfied with that approach."

The antidote to ineffective product and service development is to trade your "inside out" view for an "outside in" perspective. Start with your assumptions, as Cold Spring Granite did. As part of a LeanStrategy project, strategy team members tried to answer these questions:

- Are we among the top suppliers of our most strategic customers?
- Is the customer always right?
- Do we have a differentiated offering in each customer segment?
- Is our relationship with each key customer win-win?
- Do we have the most intimate customer knowledge in the industry?
- Does our management team spend sufficient time with strategic customers?

When they didn't like the answers, each strategy team member was given an assignment: Find a company that is clearly customer-driven and write a one-page paper describing how it performs and what it does. Presentations of the papers convinced team members they had a lot to learn. They started by choosing the top three examples and inviting principals from each company to talk to the team.

Like Cold Spring Granite, most companies have a lot to learn about what it means to be customer-driven. Unlike Cold Spring Granite, most companies never ask the questions that will reveal just how out-of-touch they are. The questions address the key characteristics of a customer-driven organization:

- *Top Supplier to Strategic Customers.* Strategic customers offer the best fit with your organization and the greatest opportunities for you to grow. They have similar visions and values, similar cultures, and plans to continually improve and grow. If you are one of their top suppliers—not just for the products/services you provide, but of *all* of the customer's suppliers—your future is linked to theirs. You are integral to their success. And, most likely, you have shut out your direct competitors.

- *Customer's Always Right.* The focus here is not on the little issues you quibble over, but on the attitude your organization has. "Inside out" regularly interprets customer complaints and issues as customer problems: They don't use the product or service correctly, or their claim isn't covered, or they didn't follow the proper channels. An "outside in" perspective looks at the same complaints and issues as golden opportunities to improve: We didn't explain how to use our product or service correctly, or every claim is covered, or every employee has the authority to resolve a customer issue. One attitude alienates customers. The other values them.

- *Differentiated Offerings.* To most companies, "differentiated" means a different color, or a slightly different design, or an extra benefit, or some other minor variation that anyone can copy because you probably copied it, too. To us and to successful companies like Vermeer, "differentiated" means you are providing a solution, not just a product or service. It means the genesis for your offering was not an existing product or service, but the unarticulated needs and the pain points of your customers. It means your value propositions address the key competitive factors you have identified personally, independently, and rigorously.

- *Win-Win Relationships.* There's been a lot of talk about win-win relationships, but we emphasize a long-term, growth-oriented focus: Move the relationship from customer-supplier to a partnership in which you have an intimate understanding of the customer's business and needs and are committed to contributing to your customer's success. In return, you get to grow with your customers.

- *Intimate Customer Knowledge.* Let's start by agreeing that every company knows its customers. You sell stuff to them. You talk to them every day. You may survey them and hold focus groups and visit them. That's knowledge, but it's not *intimate* customer knowledge. The best customer knowledge is only available to companies that regularly spend time with their customers with the sole purpose of learning how they work, what they value, and what they need. This knowledge not only drives the development of innovative solutions, but it also defines value for your organization.

- *Time Spent with Customers.* We also agree that every company spends time with its customers. The same cannot be said for senior leaders. As we noted in the last chapter, we recommend that all senior leaders spend at least one week a month with key customers. This is a challenge for most executives and one they often have trouble rationalizing. We'll provide plenty of good reasons for spending more time with customers in the pages to come.

The answers to the customer-centered questions asked by Cold Spring Granite cannot be found in marketing or sales. They won't be evident in surveys or focus groups. You won't find them in market share data or complaints to customer service.

You have to start with the customer, with matching what you offer to what your customers need and want. The lean approach to marketing differs from traditional marketing in several ways: quick and simple versus slow and elegant; direct and measurable versus indirect and immeasurable; cross-functional versus functional; waste-free versus wasteful. The differences are evident from the start in how you relate to customers.

THE POWER OF OBSERVATION

Few customers always know exactly what they want. Not many know what the options are. Ask them what they need, and they will tell you they need a better version of what they have. Their creative energy goes into what they sell, not what they buy. That's your job.

The best way to discover what your customers' need is by observing how they work in the field, at their sites, using your products/services, or those of your competitors. This is called capturing the Voice of the Customer. Let's say you want to introduce a new product or service to an existing customer group. Once you've decided which group to study, you need a team of twelve to sixteen people to discover the Voice of the Customer. The team should include senior leaders, managers, representatives from marketing and sales, and engineers or product/service developers.

The next step is to identify the "real customer," not to be confused with dealers, distributors, buyers, executives, or others who don't actually use your product or service. You will surely solicit input from these other groups, but team members need to observe how your product or service is typically used or could be used, and for that, they must watch end users.

The team compiles a list of at least six to eight companies to visit, including customers, potential customers, previous customers, and customers who use competitors' products or services. Look for happy, unhappy, and demanding customers. Marketing and sales can help you find the best candidates. For each company, identify specific people or work teams to be observed—again, those who actually use your products/services or your competitors'—and pair off team members for the visits.

Customer visits last one or two days. In our experience, people are honored that you are visiting them and delighted that you care enough about their business to listen and learn from them. The visits themselves strengthen customer relationships.

Team members need to know what they are looking for and how they should observe. We suggest the following approach:

- **Choose.** Identify the subjects of your interviews and what you want to learn from them. Consider your options:
  o Ask those who use your product or service what works well and what doesn't work at all, what prevents them from doing the best job, what compromises they have to make while using your products and services, and how they would make the product/service better.

o   Ask managers what problems cause delays, add cost, and hurt quality.

o   Ask executives/owners what features in your product/service would help their company succeed. Ask what keeps them awake at night, what problems they face as leaders beyond what your company provides.

o   Ask buyers what factors they consider, and in what priority, when purchasing products/services from you or your competitors.

o   Ask marketing and sales people what *their* customers' need, how those customers make their buying decisions, and how they are differentiating their company in the marketplace.

- *Learn.* The purpose of the visits is to learn: (1) what issues the company faces; (2) what the company needs to succeed; (3) how the company prioritizes these issues and needs; (4) how your products/services respond to those issues and needs; (5) how your products/services compare to those of competitors; (6) where the waste is in customer processes.

- *Observe.* See how customers use your product or service, or those of your competitors. Write down what you see. Use "kaizen eyes" to look for waste in what they are doing, such as unnecessary movement, excessive scrap, rework, erratic flow, bottlenecks, etc. Customers will accept a lot of waste as part of their daily routines. Don't try to solve problems during the visit, but take detailed notes—and photographs or video, if possible—to help develop solutions later.

- *Listen.* Talk to the people who use the product or service. One team member should take the lead in asking questions while both team members take notes. Let the customer talk 90 percent of the time. Write down the responses word-for-word; if possible, record the interview and have it transcribed.

- *Ask.* Before the visit, team members should prepare a list of questions to guide the interviews and their observations. They should also understand the purpose of the visit and the kind of information they seek so that they are prepared to ask follow-up questions about specific areas of interest. A curious mind will often expose new opportunities for innovation.

- **Uncover.** The people you interview cannot give you a definitive list of the features, products, or services they need. As quality guru W. Edwards Deming observed, nobody ever asked for the light bulb. While their insights are limited by their experiences and reflect only what they know, they have unarticulated needs that are also important and unmet. They have pain points that worry and frustrate and aggravate them because they don't know what to do about them. If you can uncover these unstated needs and pain points through observing and listening, you will gain a unique perspective of your customers that your competitors won't have.

Capturing the true Voice of the Customer is an active, hands-on process that is most effective when done by a diverse, internal team. It works best when team members assume they know nothing about what the customer wants because it opens their minds to new possibilities. Team members must be objective, generalized, and unbiased. They must shed their preconceived beliefs and opinions about what customers want and really listen to what they're saying and watch how they are working.

This can be particularly difficult for people from marketing, sales, and engineering. Each department has an ingrained view of the customer's world and their role in it, much like the people in production started the lean journey with an ingrained view of how to do *their* work. Like production, marketing, sales, and engineering must change the ways they work to keep the journey alive. Unlike production, these areas are not used to being watched and measured, and that will have to change. The focus of all three areas must be on increasing the time spent on value-added work and decreasing the non-value-added activities. That begins with an "outside in" view. The customer defines value. You learn how the company defines value through the Voice of the Customer.

"In the past, when we wanted to design a product, we would have marketing and engineering get together to come up with features and specifications," said Hayward Pool Products' Paul Adelberg. "We don't do that anymore. Too often, we ended up redesigning on the fly because, once we showed the new product to customers, we found out it didn't satisfy their needs. Now we get the Voice of the Customer first. Marketing people spend days and weeks traveling around the nation, gathering information, finding out what customers want to see in a new pump, what features and benefits they want."

Discovering the Voice of the Customer takes time but doesn't require big capital investments. It delivers an original vision of what your customers' need, not a ready-made view that everyone shares. When your visits are completed, you will be ready to come to your own conclusions based on your own research, and to develop innovative solutions your competitors cannot match.

VERMEER CAPTURES THE VOICE OF THE CUSTOMER

Vermeer conducted its first Voice of the Customer visits in January 2004. It wanted a new design for a horizontal directional drill, a machine used for installing gas and electric lines, water pipes, and telecommunications lines underground without excavating or digging trenches.

"Our data-gathering process lasted two weeks, like a blitz," said Kevin Alft. "We had twenty people in teams of four, divided by geographic areas. I had our CEO with me. We saw customers and non-customers, including those not using Vermeer products, or using a different process than the product we were looking at."

By observing and listening to customers, the team identified five major areas for improvement: thrust, torque, ergonomics, size, and noise. The next step involved understanding the value proposition for the customer to identify which features to create, eliminate, elevate, or decrease.

INTERPRETING THE VOICE OF THE CUSTOMER

Operational excellence is about running the same race faster, but that only gets your company so far. To grow, you must run a different race your competitors are not ready to enter. That means translating the Voice of the Customer into high-value, differentiated solutions.

When Vermeer's horizontal directional drill team concluded its customer visits, it took four days to gather and organize the notes taken by team members. "Notes" is probably not the best word, since team members wrote down everything they heard, word-for-word. The verbatim comments exposed the team to how their customers felt about their equipment.

Organizing Voice of the Customer information focuses on what the product or service must do, what elements are essential from the customers' perspective, what stands in the way of customer satisfaction/delight with the product or service, what outcomes customers' desire, and what should be maximized or minimized. To clarify these issues, Vermeer created a House of Quality.

A House of Quality is a visual tool for translating customer requirements into product or service requirements. There are eight rooms in the house, as shown in the example in Figure 5-1. Let's look at a general blueprint of what goes into each of these rooms.

1. *Customer requirements and their importance to customers.* Customers determine *what* adds value to your product or service. These requirements are listed in the first room and are the "whats" around which the House is built. The importance of each requirement is shown by ranking them in a second column.

2. *Technical requirements.* The second room describes the product or service in terms of the company by listing all of the measurable characteristics that relate to meeting the customer requirements identified in the first room. They are the "hows": *how* your company will deliver *what* your customers require.

3. *Interrelationship matrix.* The main body of the House relates customer requirements to technical requirements, the *whats* to the *hows*. The team considers each combination of customer and technical requirements to determine the level of this relationship, which is usually on a four-point scale: high, medium, low, or none. The team assigns each level a score to compare their relative value, which is listed in the seventh room.

Figure 5-1   House of Quality Example

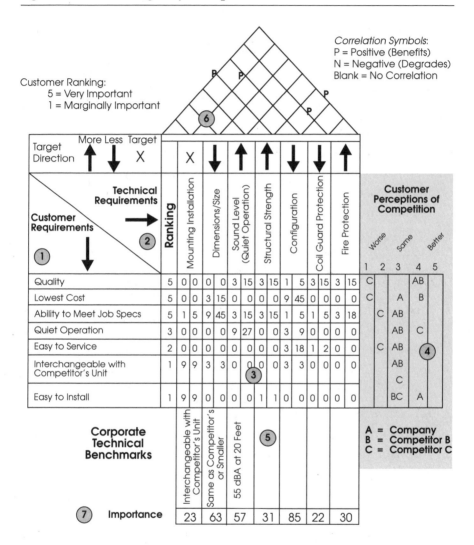

4. Competitive analysis. In this room, you compare your performance to that of your competitors on each of the customer requirements, on a scale of 1-5.

5. Benchmarks. In this room, you identify the strengths and weaknesses of key *competitors on each of the technical requirements.*

6. *Correlation matrix.* The roof of the House provides space to compare each *how* to all other *hows*. As with the interrelationship matrix, the team considers each pairing, one at a time, to determine if improving performance on one requirement would improve or hurt performance in the other. The correlations help identify where a design improvement could produce several benefits, where trade-offs must be made, and where innovation can avoid the need for compromises.

7. *Importance.* In this room, the team calculates weighted scores for each technical characteristic based on the interrelationships matrix and customer importance ratings. The ratings are the team's best estimate of which of the *hows* will have the greatest impact on customer satisfaction and provide guidance to those who will design the new product or service.

8. *Expectations or targets.* The final room, which is not included in Figure 5-1, shows the target values for the new product or service design based on the information in all other rooms, and on the team's conclusions.

Figure 5-1 is an example of a simplified, completed House of Quality. Bob Wenning, a senior management consultant for TBM, is a master contractor when it comes to helping our clients build Houses of Quality. "We do kaizen events around distilling what the team saw when it visited customers," said Bob. "We'll have countless pages of information and thousands of verbatims that we organize on flip charts around the room. We have to distill that down into families or patterns. That's the power of the process, distilling all the different things that twelve to sixteen people heard down to the top twenty-five areas. We spend a whole week doing this."

The first part of the week focuses on the organization and distillation of the Voice of the Customer information. The rest of the week is spent building a House of Quality. Even the seemingly easy steps, such as listing customer requirements in the first "room," require discussion and agreement. "If the customer says, 'I want it to be portable,' what does that mean? The team has to interpret the information it collected to figure out if 'portable' means it has wheels, or it runs on batteries, or something else," said Bob.

The team must come to consensus on the items in each "room" before moving on to the next one. That's why the process takes a week, but it's a week well-spent. The completed House of Quality captures prioritized customer requirements, technical requirements, critical features of the product or service, and expectations for what the new or redesigned product or service will deliver. More importantly, it identifies the requirements, features, and expectations that every interested party agrees are important. Such early agreement accelerates the product/service development process, as we will discuss in the next chapter. It also helps bring marketing, sales, and engineering closer.

The goal of the process is to make product and service decisions *before* the design. Once requirements are established and expectations are set, you avoid the "feature creep" that can turn a well-defined product into an Edsel. You reduce the time to market and the cost of the new product or service: Mature lean enterprises can reduce the time to market by 50 percent or more at a reduced capital investment of 50 percent or less.

You also ascertain demand before the product or service hits the market, solidifying the first part of the pull process—customer demand—to develop a lean production process that matches that demand level.

FROM PRODUCT/SERVICE TO SOLUTIONS

Initial forays into the Voice of the Customer focus on new or improved products and services, but like operational improvements, such efforts help you run the same race faster. To run a different race, you need to become a solutions provider.

A solutions provider finds the unique mix of products, services, and activities that create superior value for targeted customers. Huck Fastening Systems was a solutions provider for Boeing, providing the fasteners it needed (products), tool replacement and repair (services), and fasteners hung on the wings for easier assembly (simplification).

As with products and services, providing the right solutions begins with the Voice of the Customer. Huck Fastening Systems discovered new opportunities to serve Boeing by observing how its fasteners were used and by talking to assemblers, managers, and others involved in building airplanes. The company widened the scope of its investigations, looking beyond narrow product enhancements to innovative solutions. By understanding the obvious and the unarticulated needs of its customer, Huck Fastening Systems cemented their partnership, making it nearly impossible for competitors to step into its shoes because the boundary between it and Boeing became seamless.

Fred Heldenfels seeks the same relationship with his company's key customers. Heldenfels Enterprises makes and installs precast concrete structures for buildings. "We're trying to come up with a bundle of services and products to offer a complete solution to the market, rather than being purely product driven," said Fred. "We hope to define what our customer groups' value, their obvious needs, but we're also hoping to pick up the unarticulated needs, the problems they wish our building systems solved."

Three years into its lean journey, Heldenfels Enteprises is ready for serious growth. "We feel the transformation is more in front of us than behind us," said Fred. During the first phase of its journey, Heldenfels realized significant productivity, quality, delivery, and cost improvements. It enters the second phase with the capacity to grow and the ability to identify growth opportunities through the Voice of the Customer.

In our experience, companies in growth mode possess ten key characteristics:

1. They clearly and decisively define their business.
2. They identify specific regions for focused attention.
3. They define segments, by customer group, in the market.

4. They fully understand the key factors of competition in each market.

5. They know how competitors add value—or don't—in each segment.

6. They know what customers in each segment value, don't value, and would value if available.

7. They invent breakthrough ways to add value for customers in each segment by developing strong value propositions for key competitive factors.

8. They realign their support processes by customer group.

9. They use a cross-functional, outward-looking approach to develop a growth strategy and make it a year-round, ongoing effort.

10. They let the market speak to them.

Senior management defines the business and identifies regions and customer groups for focused attention. We will discuss value propositions, realignment, and growth strategies in Chapter 7. The knowledge of what customers' value and how you and your competitors meet their needs comes from the Voice of the Customer. Using the approaches we've described, you can gain unique insights into what your customers' need, insights you can use to differentiate the goods and services you provide, and turn a supplier relationship into a partnership.

The translation of customer needs into innovative products and services, rapidly and cost effectively, is the goal of a process we call Design for LeanSigma, which we will describe in the next chapter.

CHAPTER SIX

Developing Game-Changing Products and Services

Just as Tom Hanks declared in *A League of Their Own,* "There's no crying in baseball," most people would be quick to claim that "There's no fun in business." While that certainly describes the mindless work demanded by the old management system, it's not true in an organization immersed in a lean transformation. For many employees, the antidote of transformational management engages their minds, stirs their creativity, challenges them to learn, rewards their growth, and taps into their desire to improve. And it's fun.

A few years ago, Anand was in Germany guiding a kaizen team for a company that makes headlights for Mercedes Benz and Porsche. The company's president and head of R&D were on the team, which was studying production processes. The company could assemble a headlight in thirteen seconds. One part used in that assembly was a wire harness pulled from a big bin that came from the supplier. Every so often, the wires in the harness would get tangled and it would take the assembler a minute to untangle them, which caused the loss of three or four assembly cycles.

The team brainstormed how best to have the supplier deliver harnesses to the assembly line and came up with the idea to use a chute filled by the water spider (a lean term for the person who provides materials to the line) that can provide an untangled wire harness, thus creating predictable rhythm. The head of R&D said his group would design the chute and solve the problem within three months. Anand wanted the team to design the chute right away that day. The head of R&D resisted the idea, reminding the group that such tasks were R&D's expertise.

Anand approached the R&D leader. "How about this?" he said. "Today you're working for me." He drew a circle on the floor and had the head of R&D stand in it and watch the team construct a chute with cardboard and tape and whatever else was at hand. After an hour the R&D guy asked if he could join the activity. He sat on the floor and added his ideas to the team's and created a beautiful design. "This is fun," he later admitted. "It's like being a kid again."

We use this story to highlight two characteristics of the transformational management system that differ significantly from the scientific model. The first is how much it energizes an organization. In a traditional organization, most people know when they walk into the building, that they will subconsciously check their most human attributes at the door: curiosity, creativity, enthusiasm, passion, joy, caring. Scientific management preached that people were most efficient when they behaved like machines. What it failed to realize was that organizations are inefficient when their people act like robots.

The second difference links to the first by making it possible for people to be fully human in the workplace. The rapid and impressive improvements we've described in quality, delivery, cost, service, productivity, and financial performance are not due to huge investments in equipment, technology, or facilities; they are the result of unleashing the potential of the people in those organizations. Rather than dropping each person into a slot and limiting his or her experiences and responsibilities to a narrow area, lean organizations involve people in Voice of the Customer activities, kaizen breakthrough events, daily improvement, and a process previously reserved for specialists: product development. Based on our experiences over the past fifteen years with more than 500 organizations in different industries and cultures, organizations use no more than 20 to 30 percent of the true human potential and creativity available to them. The rest stays dormant and untapped.

IMAGINE THE POSSIBILITIES

More and more companies are coming to the same conclusion: To survive, they must accelerate the process of developing new products that meet customers' expectations and get those products to market faster, with higher quality and lower cost.

It's not a conclusion they welcome. For most companies, product development is a frustrating process that delivers disappointing results. A study by the Product Development Institute showed that more than 75 percent of companies take longer than twelve months to bring a new product to market. More than one-fourth take longer than two years, while only 7 percent get it done in less than six months.

Not only does it take too long to develop new products, a high percentage of them aren't successful, failing to meet profit, sales, and market targets. One measure of the effectiveness of a product development process is the percent of a company's total revenue and profits that comes from new products. The Product Development Institute discovered that, for companies in the bottom 20 percent in financial performance, only 8 percent of their revenue and profits came from new products, while for companies in the top 20 percent, 37 percent of revenue and 41 percent of profits came from new products. Only about a third of projects were considered successful by the poorer performers, while the top performers achieved a 79 percent success rate.

The reasons for weak product development are easy to identify:

* The company doesn't understand its customers' problems, issues, and needs . . .
* . . . but thinks it does.

- The gap between the perceptions of marketing and engineering create a lack of clarity and a lack of consensus.
- The lack of clarity, consensus, and customer information adds excessive and costly features.
- No method exists for deciding what to create, eliminate, raise, or reduce.

In the last chapter, we described how you can listen and observe to uncover unique insights by following a disciplined Voice of the Customer process. The knowledge you gain from these activities guides your product (and service—our first lean design project was for an insurance company) development process and feeds the House of Quality, which is a tool for translating customer and technical requirements into product features. However, much of this effort will be wasted without an agile, creative, and lean product development process.

We will introduce such a process, what TBM calls Design for Lean-Sigma, in this chapter. It combines the best of lean and Six Sigma to produce a rapid, robust product or service development cycle.

You've probably heard all about Six Sigma and its black belts and green belts, and the money it can help a company save. Six Sigma focuses on controlling a process to the point of plus or minus six sigma (standard deviations) from a centerline. Such control would drastically improve quality to only 3.4 defects per million opportunities. A Six Sigma program relies on a formal problem-solving framework executed by highly-skilled Black Belts and Green Belts.

We recommend combining the best of Six Sigma and lean for those complex projects like product development that would benefit from using statistical tools to handle multiple variables. Lean promotes speed, action, immediate improvement, and employee involvement. By combining the best of both, you can get the same results is a much shorter time period.

If you follow the Design for LeanSigma approach in your company, you will realize significant improvements in time to launch, expected quality, expected costs, and reduced capital requirements. But don't take our word for it.

"Through Design for LeanSigma, we've reduced the time from inception to going to market by 50 percent," said Hayward's Paul Adelberg. "By reducing the time this much, we gain the revenue more quickly and free up resources in marketing and engineering to double the amount of products we've been able to introduce. We're getting it right the first time and meeting customer expectations better."

It doesn't matter what industry you are in, what products or services you produce, or whether you have a tradition of innovation, a lean approach to product development will give your company a competitive advantage.

"Hubbell is in a very mature industry," said President and CEO Tim Powers, "so the life cycles of some of our products are up to 15 years, although the trend is for those cycles to get shorter and shorter. We want to be the clear leader in our space to differentiate ourselves from our competitors. To that end, we doubled our rate of innovation from 2001 to 2004 and we want to double it again by the end of 2006."

A lean design process capable of reducing time to market by more than 50 percent, reducing capital investments by more than 50 percent, and improving the number and profitability of new products integrates the key concepts of a company-wide lean transformation:

- It is customer driven.
- It involves employees from different functions.
- It promotes speed.
- It seeks value-added steps.
- It stimulates innovation.
- It improves quality and on-time delivery.
- It delivers dramatic results.

Here's how it works.

CREATIVITY BEFORE CAPITAL

Before the design process begins, a business case must be created to address the market to be targeted, the reasons for the new or redesigned product, projected costs and revenues, and projected timeline to launch. Upon approval of the proposal, a team leader is assigned to guide the project, which then enters the five-phase development process shown in Figure 6-1.

The stage-gated process itself is nothing new. What *is* new is the speed at which the process is completed and the results it achieves. The stimulus for rapid product development can be found in the first phase, when the Voice of the Customer is translated into product requirements, an

Figure 6-1   Phase Gate Product Development Process

Figure 6-1. Phase Gate Product Development Process

Phase 0 Market Feasibility	Phase 1 Concept Feasibility	Phase 2 Design	Phase 3 Production Preparation	Phase 4 Launch	Phase 5 Post-Launch Review	
• Develop business case • Develop preliminary financials • Assign team leader	• Select team • Develop schedule • Establish customer requirements • Conduct competitive analysis • Define spec's • Refine financials • Determine objectives • Identify suppliers/partners • Identify concept • Define risks	• Develop detailed design • Conduct first design reviews • Submit capital requests for engineering	• Review final design • Develop production process and lay out line • Draft literature • Initiate customer support training • Conduct reliability testing • Develop pre-production build • Submit production capital requests	• Order materials • Set up production line • Pilot production units • Initiate production start-up • Obtain quality first article approval	• Review financials vs. business case • Establish lead time • Define improvements to product development process	LAUNCH

(IDEA ——————→ LAUNCH arrow spanning the phases)

Toll Gate 0	Toll Gate 1	Toll Gate 2	Toll Gate 3	Toll Gate 4	Toll Gate 5
• Project approved • Team leader assigned	• Spec's. defined • Financials confirmed • Preliminary concept • Authorization to proceed	• Verification that product will meet goals • Working prototypes • Capital and tooling costs • Verification of material costs	• Review of product test performance • Release for launch	• Product released for distribution and sale	• Product corrective action • Product development process improvement

innovative concept is selected, and a consensus design is developed. Informed decisions made now, early in the process, prevent excessive changes made later, which inevitably delay delivery and add cost.

As we discussed in the last chapter, most companies assume they know what their customers' want without ever validating their perceptions. Discovering the true Voice of the Customer replaces assumptions with facts. We described how Vermeer listened to customers to redesign its small horizontal directional drills. Prior to that project, its engineers rarely interacted with customers, relying primarily on dealer input to identify product features and ending up with products that were only slightly different than those of its competitors.

Vermeer sent engineers to observe and talk to the customers of its drill. The engineers developed a clear understanding of what the customer really needed. They learned *why* the need exists, which is critical to generating innovative solutions. They also connected to the people who will use the machines, inspiring the Vermeer team to create designs that will delight their customers. The next step for Vermeer—and the first phase in the design process—involved finding innovative ways to address customer needs.

Our mantra for the first phase is *creativity before capital*. We assemble diverse, cross-functional design teams that include, but are not limited to, representatives from marketing, sales, engineering, customer service, quality, procurement, and manufacturing. We tell them to come to the design process with a "soft brain," leaving preconceived ideas behind and being open to new approaches. We give the team a short time to frame the concept, during which lots of ideas will be generated. And we tell them there's no money to spend. Creativity before capital.

We then follow a formal process for managing creativity:

1. ***Determine the function.*** What is the product or service supposed to do? The team expresses functions through word pairs, joining verbs and nouns to capture a clear thought and a simple, quick, memorable phrase. For example, the functions of a vase would be to *contain water*, *support stems*, and *display flowers*.

2. *Generate unconventional ideas.* Thomas Edison said, "To invent you
need a good imagination and a pile of junk." In this case, the "junk"
is ideas, and the more you can generate, the more the team will have
to work with. You can find ideas in a variety of places including:

- *Nature.* How are similar functions accomplished in nature? The
  purpose of this step is to force people to move away from what
  they know and to imagine new possibilities. In nature, we find
  near-perfect designs that have evolved over a very long time. For
  example, a team at Hill-Rom, a division of Hillenbrand Industries
  based in Batesville, Indiana, that provides products and services
  to healthcare facilities, was formed to reduce the noise of a fan
  that cooled electronic components under hospital beds. An engineer on the team had seen a television special on birds of prey
  that compared hawks to owls. While a diving hawk makes noise
  that is covered by daytime racket, a night owl must descend without noise, which it can do because its wings have small serrations
  along the edges that deflect airflow. The team applied this knowledge to its fan, feathering the fan blades so that they whirled
  almost silently.

- *Outside your industry.* When Kiichiro Toyoda, the founder of Toyota Motor Company, visited Ford in the 1930s, he learned how
  standardization and flow improved productivity and quality. But
  the Ford plant at River Rouge wasn't his only stop. Another key
  element of the Toyota Production System is the pull system, by
  which parts feeding an assembly line are replenished only as they
  are consumed. Toyoda got the idea for the pull system during visits to American supermarkets. Looking for ideas outside your
  industry requires a "soft brain" capable of fresh insights and unexpected connections.

  For example, we once worked with a company that manufactured caskets. They wanted to offer a low-cost model, but they
  couldn't see beyond what they were already doing. We arranged
  a tour of a local mall and instructed them to look for something

made out of sheet metal or tin that was very inexpensive. One person saw a huge tin filled with popcorn for $25. Using that concept, the team explored the idea of making a low-cost casket that appeals to people who want pictures or designs stamped into it. The result? A casket for under $200.

- *Old ideas.* Instead of filing away old ideas or designs, haul them out and post them and play with them. Figure out how and why they work and what's good and bad about them. Observe how others interact with them and imagine new uses.

3. *Create seven alternatives.* Loaded up with requirements, insights, and ideas, the team is now ready to design the product or service. This is usually when someone in the group (most likely an engineer) proposes a solution and the team, eager to make progress, nods agreement. We want to avoid that. Our goal is to engage the creativity of the group, not to jump on the first idea that comes to mind. To do this, we break the team into small groups and challenge them to come up with at least seven ideas for every critical part of the design, which have typically been determined through the House of Quality (HOQ). To fully access the creative sides of their brains, we tell them they cannot write their ideas down: They must sketch them. They have to communicate through diagrams. Figure 6-2 illustrates the rough, easy-to-understand sketches we seek.

When the small groups have completed their assignment, the entire team evaluates the alternatives based on the technical characteristics listed in the HOQ, estimated costs, and the ease with which they can be produced. The team chooses the best two or three designs and uses whatever materials are at hand to build three-dimensional models, which are then evaluated against customer requirements to select the best design.

We use a Concept Evaluation Worksheet for this purpose. On it, the team lists the HOQ technical characteristics and their relative importance on a 1-5 scale. It then rates the three proposed designs on a 0-10 scale for each characteristic, comparing them to the current design (if there

Figure 6-2   Example of Creating at Least Seven Alternatives at a Glance

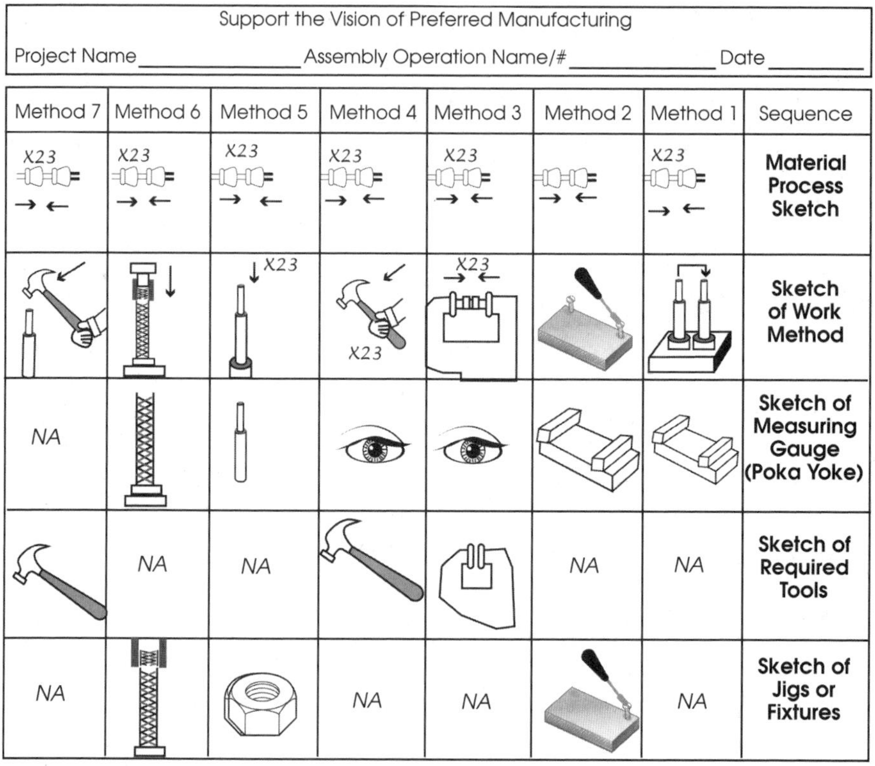

is one), which rates a baseline "5" for each characteristic. Rate times rank produces a score for each characteristic, and the totals of the scores reveal which proposed designs, if any, outperforms the current design.

DEVELOPING A "GAME-CHANGING PRODUCT"

If you've ever been in your company's computer room, you may have seen racks used to house switches, routers, and other gear and cables. They were often cobbled together by IT because nothing existed on the market to securely store components of different sizes and shapes in the smallest possible space.

Hubbell Premise Wiring had been working to solve that problem for two years with little to show for it. It decided to use Design for Lean-Sigma to jumpstart the process, using three weeklong kaizen projects to address three key areas: (1) What does the customer want? (2) What design will best serve customer and business objectives? (3) How can we manufacture it profitably?

From January to March, the business unit formally and systematically collected customer requirements and analyzed data, including polling customers through an online questionnaire. Using this information, it identified the top six features of a rack system and then asked a large group of customers to rank those features in order of importance. To the team's surprise, the feature they had ranked first was listed fifth by its customers.

By Friday of the first kaizen week, the team had a very different picture of what its end product needed to do. It also had agreement among all major players about which elements were important.

A team of fourteen people spent the second kaizen week using our formal process for managing creativity to design a new rack. They determined its critical functions, generated ideas, sketched alternatives, and evaluated the most promising designs. The winning design had 80 percent fewer parts than its predecessor, provided 10 to 15 percent more rack room, and used less valuable floor space.

The third kaizen week, which was held at the preferred vendor's site, focused on production preparation. The goal was to refine the design, optimize costs, and run through the actual manufacturing process. The team started punching metal on Wednesday and parts rolled out of the paint booth on Thursday morning, at which time the team asked local customers to review the new product. On the last day, the team reviewed cost sheets item-by-item to identify and reconsider decisions that drove up the cost. Working as a team, the group made agreements in a couple of hours that would usually take two months.

The product development cycle at Hubbell used to take twenty months or longer. The iFRAME Network Hardware Management System was rolling off the line and selling well within eleven months of Hubbell's first Voice of the Customer kaizen event. Hubbell considers it a "game-changing product," differentiating Hubbell in the marketplace and distancing it from its competitors.

SETTING THE TARGET COST

While the design process accounts for just 5 percent of final production costs, the decisions made during this process influence 70 percent of that cost. Those decisions aren't limited to product design. Hubbell devoted its third kaizen event to identifying lean approaches to producing its new rack, targeting efficiency and cost in manufacturing, equipment, and assembly.

We advise our clients to take a market-based approach to establishing the cost of their new or redesigned products. The conventional approach fixes both cost and margin: *Cost + Margin = Selling Price*. This "inside out" approach lets those who must make the product determine how much that process will cost. The selling price has less to do with customer demand and expectations than with internal cost estimates.

A market-based approach fixes the selling price and margin: *Selling Price – Margin = Target Cost*. This "outside in" approach lets the market dictate the selling price and compels those who must make the product to do so within predetermined limits. We establish selling price, margin, and target cost during Phase I of the product development process.

To keep that cost as low as possible, we advocate making capital investment decisions at each stage of a product's life cycle, rather than all at once in the beginning. This approach allows you to more closely link investments to sales, to deliver products faster than the competition throughout the product's lifetime, and to involve the production team in several cycles of learning. In addition, at every iteration of developing a new production capability, you challenge the team to reduce cost by at least 10 percent over the previous cost.

The first stage is guided by speed. Capital investments may cost relatively more, but you can afford it because your new product will demand a higher price. In the second, or mature, stage, the focus shifts to making it cheaper and more efficiently, while remaining faster than your com-

Figure 6-3   Designing for Life Cycle Stages

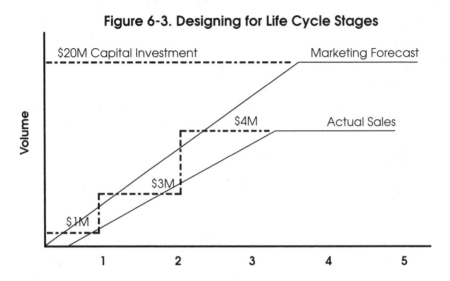

Figure 6-3. Designing for Life Cycle Stages

petitors. In the declining stage, you need to figure out how fast and cost-effectively you must make the product to realize a profit before the life cycle ends.

As the chart in Figure 6-3 shows, the three-stage approach links investments to actual sales, rather than forecasts, and that usually means smaller capital investments, more competitive prices, and profitability at every stage. Most companies cannot execute such an approach because their design processes are too slow. Lean design compresses concept, design, and production preparation, making it possible to change the manufacturing process two or three times during a product's life cycle.

DESIGNING IN QUALITY

An innovative product design can meet customer and technical requirements and cost targets and still fall short of expectations if the process and equipment needed to produce it are an afterthought. The design phase of the Design for LeanSigma process doesn't stop with the design of the product; it also addresses how the product will be made. Production preparation, or 2P, is the third phase of the design process and is often centered around one or more weeklong kaizen events.

In the case of Vermeer's horizontal directional drill, the launch team held several week-long 2P events to develop manufacturing processes and refine the product design. The first events focused on creating fishbone diagrams that showed the proposed sub-assemblies and how the components should flow toward final assembly, producing mock-ups and sketches to define and illustrate the function of tooling, listing special tooling and equipment, and scheduling its construction and tryout dates. Subsequent "fit and function" 2P events modified the product design and production process based on the assembly of two prototypes. In the assembly pilot 2P event, Vermeer built five pre-production trial units, collecting actual cycle times for all assembly processes, completing labor balancing to determine the number of employees needed, finalizing assembly standard work manuals, finalizing the bill of material, and verifying the production readiness of the tooling and equipment.

As Vermeer's experience suggests, several lean concepts are applied to make sure the product can be manufactured as fast as possible, with the highest quality, and at the lowest cost:

- *One-piece flow.* The end point for any new product is customer demand. In a lean production environment, nothing is made until that demand kicks in and something is bought. The opposite of manufacturing large batches of products, which grow inventory and hide problems, one-piece flow focuses on building products only in response to demand. The continuous flow of work one piece at a time reveals waste and other problems, improves quality and productivity, reduces inventory, opens up floor space, promotes flexibility, and improves safety and morale.

- *Mistake proofing.* In every process there is the potential for errors to be made. If you wait to find and correct defects caused by these errors, quality, delivery, and cost will suffer. Mistake proofing, which was originally developed by Shegio Shingo and called *poka yoke*, is a technique for avoiding and eliminating errors, in this case through controls in the product, or in the production process, that prevent errors from occurring. Mistake-proofing techniques include designing out an unnecessary activity, substituting a more reliable and creative approach without spending much money, making it impossible to make a mistake, and making an activity easier to perform.

- *Defect detection.* Not all errors can be prevented, which is why you must develop conditions for immediate detection and responses to abnormal conditions within the production process. The goal is to prevent a defective product from being passed to the next operation. This technique, called jidoka or autonomation, requires guidelines for when and how the line will be stopped, and the assignment of roles and responsibilities for stopping the line and responding with countermeasures.

- *Standard work and standardized WIP.* As production is matched to customer demand and the steps in the process are defined, the proper sequence must be visualized, documented, and posted to ensure consistent performance and to keep people from reverting to old habits. This is called standard work, and it helps in the training of new operators to immediately follow the minimum, reliable steps required to repeat work without abnormalities. Standard work-in-process (WIP) is the minimum amount of work-in-process required to complete the work sequence on demand.

- *Standardized parts.* Too many unique parts clutter the work area, requiring multiple batches of parts and multiple tools for installing them. Anand remembers proudly showing Shigeo Shingo, the engineering genius who helped develop many of the manufacturing methods that are part of the Toyota Production System, a production process that Anand and his team had taken down from eight hours to one hour. Shingo noticed that the cover plate for the product was secured by sixteen screws. He asked why. Anand told him the screws were necessary to hold the cover plate in place. Shingo showed how one screw on top would accomplish the same thing and would reduce assembly and repair time. "Every screw that has to be taken out and put back takes thirty seconds," he said. "There are sixteen screws so that's eight minutes being wasted." Anand changed the design.

- **Ease of assembly.** Designing for ease of assembly means considering how parts are presented to the assembler, handled, inserted, and fastened to facilitate simple patterns of movement in a minimal space. This includes redesigning parts that could become tangled, seeking symmetry so that a part doesn't have to be oriented a certain way, assembling vertically rather than on multiple faces of the base, and redesigning the configuration to eliminate restricted access to components. As Albert Einstein said, "The best design is the simplest design that works."

The best time to act on these concepts is during the second and third phases of the product development process (see Figure 6-1), when the parts used to assemble the product are still being finalized, the production process is still being developed, and the opportunities to reduce costs, improve productivity, and enhance quality are greatest.

THE BENEFITS OF LEAN DESIGN

Marvair is a leading manufacturer of heating, ventilation, and air conditioning equipment for commercial and specialty applications, including schools, telecommunications shelters, and commercial modular structures. This last area posed a problem for Marvair: It had just 3 percent of one market segment and its modular units cost 4 percent more than the market share leaders. Since it didn't want to get out of the business, it determined that an innovative new design costing 6.25 percent less than the competition would increase its market share. Using the market-based approach we described earlier in this chapter, the company subtracted its margin from the target price to get the target cost for the new product. The target cost dictated that Marvair had to reduce material cost by 28 percent, labor cost by 29 percent, and overhead expense by 12.5 percent. It wanted to release the new product in six months and get 30 percent of the market.

To help Marvair achieve these ambitious goals, we facilitated a Design for LeanSigma process. Marvair identified the customer needs and technical characteristics and constructed a House of Quality. During a product concept kaizen event, the team compared the current design to a theoretical best design, defined opportunities for the new concept, and used managed creativity to come up with innovative concepts. The team chose the two best concepts, built and evaluated mock-ups of each, and selected the most promising.

A second kaizen event focused on production preparation. In one week, the team identified and addressed potential manufacturing constraints, balanced work to achieve flow, created standard work and posted it, modified workstations and parts carts to maximize productivity, made sure all operations were ergonomically correct, and reviewed all assemblies and parts for labor or material savings. The new assembly line was laid out and set up using resources freed up by previous kaizen events, which meant no capital expenses were required. Production on the new assembly line was simulated to find and fix hidden issues and to ensure performance to goals.

The results of Marvair's lean design process affirm its effectiveness:

- Material costs reduced by 15 percent
- Labor costs reduced by 63 percent
- Overhead expenses reduced by 63 percent
- Total cost goals exceeded by 24 percent
- From concept to cash in less than eight months
- Gained the competitive advantage necessary to take market share from the competition

Hayward Pool Products discovered an unexpected benefit of lean design. "We had identified a product that we were going to build offshore because we thought it would be more cost effective," said Paul Adelberg. "We used Design for LeanSigma to find the Voice of the Customer, achieve one-piece flow, simplify the product, and get commonality of parts. At the end of the kaizen week, we found it was more cost effective to produce it here than offshore. If lean design hadn't taken away all of the price advantages, we'd be building it in China. And now we don't have to worry about lead times and inventory."

A NEW WAY OF THINKING

The lean design process succeeds for the same reasons the lean transformation succeeds: It involves employees in learning and responding to the Voice of the Customer, it provides a disciplined approach to unleashing their creativity, and it challenges them to find innovative solutions to old problems and new opportunities. It values *creativity before capital*. Those who participate on lean design teams frequently admit that they had no idea of the hassles their designs caused, or the real issues their customers' face.

The antidote of the transformational management system changes how people think, whether those people work in engineering, marketing, sales, production, or administration. It empowers people to get involved in improving their processes. It motivates them to learn and grow as individuals and as contributors to the organization. It nurtures the creativity they all possess but have rarely used. It breaks down barriers between units by focusing everyone on common goals. And it replaces apathy and boredom with enthusiasm and joy as employees commit themselves to the journey.

Once you start this transformation, you can't take it back. If leaders lose interest or drop it for something else, those employees who took part in the transformation will become disillusioned and cynical. If you believe in the power of your people to transform your company, you stay the course, and as we've seen, your company will succeed.

CHAPTER SEVEN

Becoming an Innovative Solutions Provider

If you believe your company exists to be better at something that somebody else is already doing, this chapter may not be very helpful. On the other hand, if you wonder whether your company can continue to exist by playing the same game as your competitors, this chapter is vital to your company's future.

Experts warn that an inside-out supply strategy is outdated. As Michael Gerster at WIKA said, "The old system of 'we make stuff, you buy stuff' is over." Consumers have become more demanding, expecting those who provide their products and services to listen to their needs and anticipate their desires. They demand innovation, responsiveness, and personalized solutions. The demand directly affects those who sell to consumers and ripples through their supply chains. The focus of innovation is shifting from the supply side, from an inside out attention to product and service features, to the demand side and the Voice of the Customer.

In a demand economy, a company exists to solve customer problems. This outside in perspective smashes the narrow product/service mentality that drives most organizations:

- *Supply strategy* companies rely on existing capabilities to design, produce, and sell products and services for existing customer needs. Let's say your company sells office products and services to businesses. Your supply strategy defines your offerings as pens, paper, files, printers, software, telephones, and other tangible products. When you look to grow your business, you expand into similar areas such as office furniture and printing/copying services. Your business is defined by what your company typically sells, what your customers typically buy, and what your competitors offer.
- *Demand strategy* companies rely on innovation to differentiate their products and services from those of their competitors, but they don't stop at a narrow definition of existing needs. If you work for a demand strategy office supply company, you identify key customer segments and spend time with members of each segment, watching them work and listening to their concerns. Let's say you learn that your small business customers' biggest issues are the cost of health care, saving energy, and getting their technology to work right. None of these is your company's area of expertise, but that doesn't stop you. You partner with a national health care provider to offer a health insurance plan tailored to small businesses. You design an energy saving program that teaches small businesses how to use energy more efficiently, including which energy-saving products to buy at your stores. You offer reliable technology support that guarantees everything will work as expected, whether your stores sell it or not. Your business is defined by what your customers need to succeed and grow.

A lot of people at the office supply company would wave red flags the first time they heard what demand strategy meant. "We're not an insurance company," they would object. "We're hardly experts in energy efficiency," they would argue. "We're not about to get into tech support," they would say. "Others are already doing this and doing it better than we could, so we're better off sticking to our core competencies."

Such protests are weak. First, if somebody was already meeting these needs well, they wouldn't show up in your Voice of the Customer activities as critical needs. Second, you need not be experts in these new competencies, you just have to find other companies that are and partner with them. Third, why does your company exist? If your products and services define you, wave those red flags. If customer needs define you, put them in your pocket and get to work.

Because you want to be a solutions provider. Consider our office supply company. If its customers could get office products from you but they could also save money on health insurance, use energy more efficiently, and have their technology working properly—and they couldn't get anything but office supplies from your competitors—you have a serious competitive advantage. You will build loyalty. You can lock customers in. You will be able to charge more. You will revolutionize your industry, leap ahead of the competition, and lead a very different race.

We call this value innovation, and it's the linchpin of Phase III of the new transformational management system.

LEVERAGING LEAN FOR GROWTH

Value innovation doesn't replace product innovation any more than product innovation replaces operational excellence. Each phase builds on the previous phase, and you can't jump to Phase III without mastering Phases I and II first.

The amazing discovery is that your company can gain a competitive advantage in each phase. In Phase I, you make processes more efficient to improve quality, accelerate delivery, and control costs. Such operational excellence differentiates you from your competitors and directly affects your bottom line performance.

With your operational management system under control, your company can synchronize the supply and demand chains to better understand and respond to the Voice of the Customer. In Phase II, your product and service innovations strengthen customer relationships and grow market share.

You are now ready to leverage lean for growth. In Phase III, your company becomes a solutions provider, using value innovation to compete in a unique way, earn brand loyalty, lock in customers, and take a commanding lead in a very different race.

Becoming a solutions provider means bundling activities, services, and products to create superior value for your targeted customers. The right mix can create needs your customers never knew they had. Done correctly, it can create barriers that are much more difficult for your competition to overcome and make price a relative non-issue.

A properly executed solutions provider strategy means your company, your assets, and your people become intertwined with those of your targeted customers. Few, if any, of your competitors can quickly step into your shoes, because the boundary between your own operations and those of your customers' is seamless.

We described Gary's work with Huck Fastening Systems in Chapter 5. If you simply produce fasteners for commercial aircraft makers, any fastener supplier could take your place. If you choose instead to be a solutions provider to aircraft makers, you may also provide installation tools, service the tools on the assembly line, deliver fasteners pre-kitted directly to the assembly line in the order the structures are being assembled, replenish inventory as consumed, add your own engineers to their engineering team in charge of joining systems, and participate in each other's kaizen events. Do all this and you are not just another supplier but a valued partner, and the line that separates your company from your customer is hard to find—especially for your competitors.

The line fades to invisible for your employees as well. If there is little daylight between you and your customers, your entire organization knows what is most valued: the customers' needs. When companies adopt this strategy, we see a subtle but growing shift in employees' attitudes. The customer's voice becomes louder than any other, and every employee hears it and strives to do something of value for the customer.

A solutions provider strategy helps you take more waste out of the external areas of the value chain and capture more of the profit in it. Dealers, distributors, and other channel partners often mask the real opportunities to bring value-added solutions to targeted customers. They can be mistaken for the real customer and siphon off an unjustifiable share of the profit available in the value chain.

A VALUE INNOVATOR'S VIEW OF THE MARKET

The classic view of markets holds that cost leaders and differentiators rule the fringes of the bell curve with everyone else stuck in the middle (Figure 7-1). As time goes by and competitors erode the advantages of the cost leaders and differentiators, the middle grows. Value innovators look for ways to capture the share that becomes available when the outsiders lose their edge. They use the cost advantages and differentiation strategies gained during Phases I and II to take the expanding middle ground.

Value innovation allows you to distance your company from the competition through two complementary initiatives: becoming a solutions provider, and delivering radically superior value at a low cost. It's the "sweet spot" where customer needs, buyer value, and competitive price meet. Once you claim that spot, your competitors will be hard-pressed to take it from you.

Figure 7-1   The Value Innovation Edge

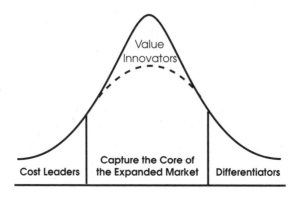

Huck Fastening Systems found the "sweet spot" with its aerospace customers. In Chapter 3, we described how Ventana Medical Systems brings value innovation to its laboratory customers through its lean lab of the future. None of its competitors offers the same bundle of products and services. "As long as we provide the total solution, it makes it extremely difficult for customers to justify buying a competitor's less costly instrument when they know they give up better delivery, better customer care, better access to diagnostics—they give up the whole solution," said T.J. Johnson, senior vice president of corporate development and manufacturing operations. "That's a huge competitive advantage for us."

For other companies, the "sweet spot" is a revolutionary approach to a traditional market, such as hotels and airlines.

Professor Ben Bensaou of Insead Institute in France studied how Hotel Formule 1 achieved profit margins of twice the industry average and occupancy rates three times the average. He identified the key factors of competition and compared the relative offerings of Formule 1 with those of its primary competitors, which are one-star and two-star hotels. Figure 7-2 shows the value curves indicating the relative level of performance provided for each key factor of competition.

As you can see, Formule 1 offers less than a one-star hotel on most of the key factors that are not valued by its targeted group of customers— road warrior sales reps. It outperforms its competition, however, in the three areas highly valued by the same customer group: bed quality, hygiene, and silence.

Formule 1 identified its target customers and then it studied them using Voice of the Customer techniques to learn what they wanted, to uncover their unarticulated needs, and to prioritize the key factors of competition. It learned that bed quality, hygiene, and silence drove customer satisfaction, that prices had to be competitive, and that the other factors had little impact on which hotel its targeted customers selected. So Formule 1 decided not to offer eating facilities, or a twenty-four-hour receptionist, or room amenities. It designed its buildings and rooms to be cost-efficient, rather than large and aesthetically appealing. These decisions helped it control costs, offer competitive prices, and increase profits.

Figure 7-2   Hotel Formule1 Value Curve

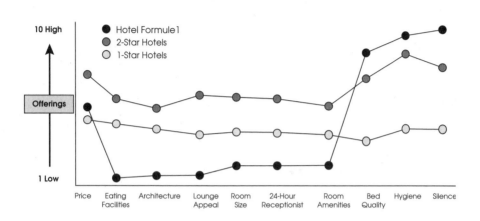

Formule1's cost per room is almost one-third that of its competitors. Its cost of staff is 20 to 23 percent, compared to 25 to 35 percent for the competition. Yet in the areas that matter most—bed quality, hygiene, and silence—Formule1 performs better than the average two-star hotel.

By reframing its strategic logic, Formule1 found the "sweet spot" in France's low-cost hotel market. To find your target markets' "sweet spots," we encourage you to discuss how your company answers the following questions—and how changing your answers might alter your competitive position:

- Do you take industry conditions as a given and let them frame your range of what is possible, or do you challenge the inevitable nature of those conditions?
- Is your focus on outpacing the competition, or creating a radically new and superior value curve that will let you dominate the market?
- Do you focus on customer segmentation and retention, or do you search for deeper and unarticulated customer needs to unlock the mass of buyers, even if that means willingly letting some existing customers go?

Figure 7-3 Southwest Airlines Value Curve

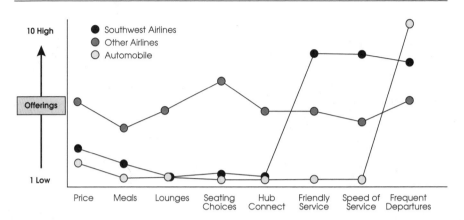

- Do you strive to improve your products and services to be best-in-class in your industry, or to provide innovative solutions to chosen customers?

One company that came up with unorthodox answers is Southwest Airlines. Instead of adopting the accepted wisdom of its legacy airline competitors, Southwest studied air travelers and came to its own conclusions. As Southwest's value curve shows, it learned that it could offer superior value at a low cost to its targeted customers, non-business travelers, by excelling at friendly service, speed of service, frequent departures, and price (Figure 7-3). It also decided that meals, lounges, seating choices, and hub connectivity were less important and were sources of cost savings.

Airlines measure cost and revenue by cents per available seat mile (ASM). According to Michael Porter, a leading authority on competitive strategy and Bishop William Lawrence University Professor at Harvard Business School, from 1998 to 2000, it cost Southwest $.0244 less per ASM than the airline industry average. As a result, Southwest charged $.0172 less per ASM than the airline industry average, while enjoying a higher operating profit. Its lower costs and higher profits forever altered the airline "race," and made Southwest the new model to emulate.

To gain a unique advantage in your marketplace, your company must develop a value proposition that finds the "sweet spot" of value, price, and cost. The value proposition must be executed with speed through integrated activities that take advantage of your Phase I and Phase II capabilities. By achieving operational excellence, you cannot be imitated, although operational excellence alone won't generate long-term growth. By internalizing the Voice of the Customer, you build market share, although synchronizing your demand and supply chains alone won't redefine your industry. Value innovation builds on these accomplishments in the first two phases of your lean journey, leveraging lean for dramatic, sustainable growth.

LEADING THROUGH VALUE INNOVATION

What we're talking about is becoming a customer-driven company. Not engineering- or marketing-driven. Not shareholder-driven. Not product-driven. Not industry- or competitor- driven. Not even leadership-driven.

Customer-driven.

To become a customer-driven company, you must become a solutions provider, using value innovation to redefine who you serve and how you serve them. As Mary Andringa, president and CEO of Vermeer, said, "Value innovation is looking for the gaps, what do customers' need that no one's providing. The goal of our value innovation strategy and work is top-line growth, sales growth, and market share gain."

We've worked with Vermeer and others to help them use value innovation to become solutions providers. This is the ten-step process we prescribe:

1. Define targeted customers.
2. Determine customer needs.
3. Analyze competitive offerings.
4. Assess distribution channels.

5. Develop differentiated solutions.

6. Create value proposition.

7. Choose a profit model.

8. Deploy the solutions.

9. Measure performance.

10. Review, align, and execute.

STEP 1: DEFINE YOUR TARGETED CUSTOMERS

The most effective solutions respond to the unique needs of specific customer groups. In the examples we've cited in this chapter, the office supply company's solutions for small businesses would not appeal to larger companies, the fastener solution for aerospace customers would not be appropriate for other types of assembly, Formule1's value curve isn't relevant to people seeking four-star hotels, and Southwest isn't targeting customers who want first-class seats and lounges in major airports. In each of these examples, the companies *could* develop solutions for a wider market, but at what cost? Feature creep leads to higher costs, poorer quality, slower delivery, and not much of a competitive advantage.

The proper segmentation of your markets depends on your ability to figure out what your customers' do and do not value. Start with existing knowledge and perceptions. Collect all the documented, usable information that exists about customers and competitors. Use the Internet to gain deeper insights into your customers and competitors. Implement the Voice of the Customer techniques we discussed in Chapter 5 to help you uncover unarticulated needs, narrow the list of key factors of competition as Formule1 and Southwest did, and prioritize those factors from the customers' perspective.

Building this internal capability requires close customer relationships and creativity. It also requires an objective, generalized, and unbiased mindset that sheds preconceived beliefs and opinions and welcomes the true Voice of the Customer. Open-ended questions reveal what matters to your customers: "What are the top two or three success factors for you in regards to the products and services you use?" If you ask this and other open-ended questions to a large enough sampling of customers in your targeted group, you will collect the information you need to create a list of the key factors of competition.

Vermeer's desire to become a solutions provider led it to develop its market-based strategy and a customized database to collect and organize information about its key customer groups. "We've been doing market-based strategy work for one year and we've got fourteen different value innovation curves we're populating," said Glenda Vander Wilt, continuous improvement manager of market-based strategy at Vermeer. "I think it's often difficult for customers to express what their problems are because they accept them as market or economic conditions. So we ask what inefficiencies they incur, what affects their profitability, what's their biggest expense?"

Each online value innovation curve includes how many contacts are in that database, the key factors of competition, and competitors and how they rate on the factors. "I can enter an unstructured interview from a discussion with a customer into the database and it automatically goes into a queue and is analyzed, and everything gets tied back," said Mary Andringa. "That's how we summarize the data."

Vermeer gets customer information from face-to-face interviews at customers' offices, job sites, and trade shows. It does telephone cold-calling of both customers and non-customers to talk about their needs and the direction of the industry. It goes to Internet chat rooms to see what people are saying about Vermeer and its competitors. And it organizes the information it gets from these and other sources in its online databases.

STEP 2: DETERMINE CUSTOMER NEEDS

There are two levels of determination to consider.

If your company wants to be a solutions provider, the first level of customer need is the bundle of products, services, and activities that address their most pressing concerns. Identifying these needs means looking beyond single products or product lines. It means observing not just how customers use your products and services, but how they function as organizations. What do they need most to be successful? Where are their pain points? What are they compromising on? What do *their* customers need? Vermeer seeks to answer these questions through its market-based strategy, capturing the broader "solution" needs in value innovation curves.

The second level of customer need focuses on specific products or services. In Chapter 5, we described how Vermeer identified customer needs related to its small horizontal directional drills. Through extensive interviews and close observation, Vermeer discovered several attributes that would greatly influence the buying decision, including a significantly higher ratio of power to machine size, rack-and-pinion drive instead of chain drive, mechanical control rather than electronics, and making it easier for operators to keep their hands on the controls.

Vermeer's ability to uncover and meet these needs, not all of which its customers could articulate, propelled its new products to industry leadership in the same way that the success of Formule1 and Southwest hinged on their interpretation of customer needs. Chapter 5 describes how to identify these needs.

STEP 3: ANALYZE COMPETITIVE OFFERINGS

Too often, companies pay little attention to their competitors in each market segment. You need to be clear about what they offer, how they offer it, and whether or not they are profitable.

The key is to gather actual data about your competition, rather than relying on anecdotes or gossip. Once you know the details about what your competitors do and how they do it, you can compare their offerings to the key factors of competition, as Vermeer has done, and to the customers' needs. "With our market-based strategy, we get in contact with end customers, understand their markets, determine the key factors of competition and how they value each factor, and identify the gaps," said Mary Andringa. "It helps us see strategic opportunities."

A company cannot see strategic opportunities without accurate knowledge of its competitors.

STEP 4: ASSESS DISTRIBUTION CHANNELS

Your role as a solutions provider extends to the total customer experience. If dealers and/or distributors own pieces of that experience, you need to understand how they will add value to your solutions—and how they won't. That means challenging the existing paradigms and exploring creative new approaches that will develop a value-adding distribution channel.

For some companies, direct access to customers is discouraged by dealers and distributors who aggressively protect their customer relationships. Guarding those relationships may not add value to your solutions, but it is invaluable for the distribution channel. Your Voice of the Customer experiences will establish your own customer connections. As a result, you will usually know more about your market segments than even the most established of your distribution channel partners.

Knowledge of your customers, competitors, and solutions can help you redefine the purpose of your distribution channel. The criteria are simple: Does it add value to your solution and align with your goals? If the answer is "yes," you have partners in your quest to become the leading solutions provider.

STEP 5: DEVELOP DIFFERENTIATED SOLUTIONS

You are now ready to create a value innovation curve for your target market. Start with the key factors of competition along the y axis. Plot the customer value for each factor, as shown in Figures 7-2 and 7-3, which you learned during Step 2.

Next, plot your company's performance and the performance of key competitors for each factor.

If you end up with a chart that looks like the Formule1 and Southwest charts, the opportunities will be easy to spot. Gaps between customers' most critical needs and the ability of competitors' offerings to meet those needs—the "white spaces" on the curve—are the "sweet spots" you want to hit. If there are more "sweet spots" than you can handle, they must be evaluated based on whether closing the gap will change the basis of competition, industry economics, or customer expectations. A strategy that changes one of these is great; a strategy that changes all three puts your company in the lead of a different race.

The white spaces between customer needs and current offerings are not the only potential sources of differentiation. Take another look at the value curves for Formule1 and Southwest. Not only did these two companies identify the most important factors of competition and set new standards in those areas, but they also *reduced* or *eliminated* their efforts on those factors that customers' considered unimportant. Their decision to do less in these areas freed up resources to do better on the most important factors, offer very competitive prices, and increase their margins.

Every product or service feature costs money. "If you just throw features at a machine, all you end up with is a too-expensive machine," said Kevin Alft, vice president of Underground Installation Solutions at Vermeer. "It's really understanding the value proposition for the customer. You have to identify what to eliminate, decrease, elevate, and create."

Once you've identified the key factors of competition, ask these questions:

- What factors should be created that the industry has never offered?
- What factors should be raised well beyond the industry standard?
- What factors should be reduced below the industry standard?
- What factors should be eliminated that the industry has taken for granted?

While answering the first two questions tends to be easy, answering the last two is not. There's a perception that you must offer everything your competitors' offer, or your customers will abandon you. Yet if you look at the success of Formule1 and Southwest, you find from four to six key factors that they reduced or eliminated. Those decisions had the opposite impact, increasing profitability and market share for both companies.

Make no mistake, the debate about reducing or eliminating features is usually intense. Marketing, sales, your distribution channel partners, and others will argue that you cannot offer less than your competitors and hope to increase sales. Your only defense is a profound knowledge of targeted customer needs and a clear understanding of what you can gain by reducing or eliminating certain features. Such knowledge and understanding will guide you to differentiated solutions no competitor can match.

STEP 6: CREATE VALUE PROPOSITIONS

Your value proposition determines if you will receive adequate revenue for the value created by the solutions you offer. In a format that could be used as a selling tool, it defines what value customers will receive and includes:

- Economic or financial benefit (saves time, labor, material, scrap/ waste)
- Convenience (requires less effort than the current product or service)
- Safety (reduces lost time or injuries)
- Environmental awareness (exceeds current regulations or meets likely future ones)
- Customer-centricity (value using customer data)
- Value propositions for your customer and your customers' customers, if possible

STEP 7: CHOOSE A PROFIT MODEL

You must identify how profits will be earned from the solutions offered. Here are twenty-two options to consider (from *Succeeding in the Changing World of Business,* author and publisher unknown):

- *Customer Solutions*: Know the customer, create a solution, develop the relationship.
- *Product Pyramid*: Offer low-price, high-volume products and high-price, low-volume products, and everything in between.
- *Multicomponent*: Sell multiple components within a system.
- *Switchboard*: Become a high-value intermediary between multiple sellers and multiple buyers.

- **Time**: Be the first to market with a unique offering.
- **Blockbuster**: Profit from blockbuster projects to pay development costs.
- **Profit Multiplier Model**: Replicate Disney's success with Mickey and Minnie.
- **Entrepreneurial**: Organize into small profit centers.
- **Specialization**: Meet the needs of a particular market segment.
- **Installed Base**: Profit from follow-on products/services to an installed base.
- **De Facto Standard**: Hold the standard for your industry.
- **Brand**: Establish a brand that customers will pay premium prices to own.
- **Specialty Product**: Introduce a new product that will take years for competitors to imitate.
- **Local Leadership**: Focus on growing local market share.
- **Transaction Scale**: In transaction-based industries, control the largest transactions.
- **Value Chain Position**: Concentrate on the areas of the value chain where profit is concentrated.
- **Cycle**: Understand your industry's cyclical behavior to create a cost or pricing edge at key points.
- **After-Sale**: Find profit further along the value stream.
- **New Product**: Take leadership of the next-generation products and services.
- **Relative Market Share**: The greater your's is relative to your competitor's, the greater your profitability.
- **Experience Curve**: Take advantage of your areas of expertise.
- **Low-Cost Business Design**: Use the lean transformation to compete while spending less.

STEP 8: DEPLOY THE SOLUTIONS

Your solutions must be created and offered through the precision of very detailed and disciplined project management. Because alignment is critical, we recommend using policy deployment, which we described in Chapter 4.

STEP 9: MEASURE PERFORMANCE

To assess the effectiveness of your solutions, you need goals, milestones, and metrics.

First, determine what levels of performance and financial impact your solutions should have in three months, six months, nine months, and one year.

Next, set dates for deciding what is and is not working. At a minimum, every week you need to know if things are getting done when they are supposed to be done and if the results are what you expected.

Finally, you must identify measures that reflect the real expectations for your solutions. This is how progress can be objectively determined.

STEP 10: REVIEW, ALIGN, AND EXECUTE

Senior leaders and others responsible for the solutions use the goals, milestones, and metrics to review, align, and execute the strategy. At weekly meetings, they evaluate performance on key measures and initiate countermeasures as needed. If subsequent meetings indicate that the countermeasures aren't working, leaders can make course corrections before too much time has passed.

Executing a solutions provider strategy that will change the competitive landscape is no time to be too forgiving of deadlines that slip or goals that are missed.

VALUE INNOVATION AT MAYTAG SERVICES

You may remember the television commercials that used the lonely Maytag repairman to tout the quality of Maytag appliances. Maytag built its service operation to handle warranty work. In 2002, a small group within Maytag asked if the company might be able to profit from turning its service capability into a business.

It started with the Voice of the Customer, studying consumer, customer, and marketplace needs. Maytag learned that the number of independent servicing companies was rapidly declining, from almost 19,000 in 1992 to 11,000 in 2004. The number of new service technicians joining the workforce each year was not meeting demand. Hotels and restaurants had trouble getting reliable service. Retailers lost money on their service business and hated the hassles. Customers wanted good quality service for all appliance types and brands at reasonable prices, with the right part in the right place at the right time.

Maytag analyzed companies already providing this service and found that neither consumers nor customers were satisfied, that the response was often quick, but follow-up calls were frequently needed, and that nobody provided "end-to-end" service.

It looked at its own capabilities, primarily its national network of repair experts that put 71 percent of American households within range of Maytag service. It saw that nearly all of its competitors had gotten out of the service business, leaving a vacuum that only one large company, Sears, and a shrinking number of independent servicing companies struggled to fill.

Maytag decided that the opportunity to provide a broader solution existed. It created Maytag Services.

Based on its knowledge of customer needs, competitor offerings, and internal capabilities, Maytag Services shifted from a Maytag warranty repair business to an all-brand service model. It developed a 48/95 target: 95 percent of the time a repair will be completed within 48 hours. It used kaizen breakthrough events to make its service people more efficient, having parts couriered to their trucks every night for the next day and eliminating the need for daily trips to service branches. It also equipped each service technician with a wireless handheld unit that gets a satellite download of each technician's daily appointment schedules, provides GPS directions for each call, and provides real-time credit card authorization and changes in schedules. To meet the growing need for service technicians, it developed a "BootCamp" process to develop new technicians through a four-week training program.

The early success of Maytag Services encouraged it to broaden its scope. "It's almost mind-boggling what the opportunities are," said Art Learmonth, president of Maytag Services. "You have to prioritize them because there are so many. For example, Samsung is now selling appliances and it had no service function, so we became its turnkey solution. Third-party companies that sell extended warranties either have to manage a network of independents, or they can come to us and get 100 percent coverage in the U.S. and Canada. Nobody serviced packaged terminal air conditioners for hotels until we offered end-to-end service. Restaurant chains find that if a local branch has a problem with a stove, it has to call one guy, but if it's a dishwasher, it's a different person, so we started a commercial business."

As the total solutions provider for consumers, manufacturers, third-party companies, retailers, hotels, restaurant chains, fitness centers, and others, Maytag Services has become the leader of a race it created. It has nearly quadrupled its number of technicians since 2001, with seven times the number of income-producing service calls it had that year. The achievements attest to Learmonth's leadership philosophy. "Number one, I surround myself with really good people," he said. "Number two, I set very aggressive goals. And number three, I get out of the way."

YOUR OPPORTUNITIES FOR GROWTH

To leverage lean for growth, you need to find the right platform that fits your company's vision, capabilities, traditions, and competitive environment, and your people must have the resources and responsibilities to attack growth projects. Maytag Services aggressively pursued several growth platforms that fit its vision and capabilities, provided training and technological resources to fuel the growth, and delegated responsibility to those involved in the process.

As your company enters the growth phase of its lean transformation, here are six growth platforms that can provide a framework for a regular scan for opportunities:

- **Products/Services.** Sell new products and services to existing customers, or modify current products/services to attract new customers.
- **Markets.** Expand your geographical reach with new or existing products.
- **Channels.** Create differentiated solutions specific to channel opportunities and create aftermarket opportunities for your channel partners.
- **Acquisitions.** Look for complementary products and services, going narrow and deep when adding to product lines.
- **Value Chain.** Take ownership of outsourced pieces of the value chain, such as distribution or raw materials.
- **Business Model.** Open up a new view of your business.

In the next chapter, we will propose a plan your company can follow to go from where it is today to a position of industry leadership similar to that achieved by Vermeer, Maytag Services, and others. The roadmap begins, as it must, by focusing on internal processes and the steps you can take to speed them up, improve quality, and squeeze out costs. The roadmap then extends outward to customers and suppliers, and to new opportunities made possible by the resources saved during Phase I. Armed with operational excellence and aligned demand and supply chains, you are prepared to leverage lean for growth and distinguish yourself from the competition.

CHAPTER EIGHT
Putting It All Together

The late comedian Sam Kinison once remarked that whenever he got the urge to exercise, he read a book about exercise until the urge passed.

Since the thought of transforming a company is a far more daunting prospect, we want to help you get started before the urge passes. We've introduced a number of concepts in the first seven chapters and shared other companies' experiences and, hopefully, convinced you that your old management system is outdated and a new one is in your company's best interests.

But we don't want you to wait. The lean journey is an action-oriented experience that values speed. It's a "ready-fire-aim" kind of approach. "The whole concept of kaizen is, if this doesn't work we'll try something else until we find something that *does* work," said Barb King of Landscape Structures. "No idea is a bad idea, and we can change, and we're not going to break the company by doing it."

In this chapter, we lay out a standard approach to transforming your organization by integrating the new management system. While you will want to customize it to your unique situation, the key elements remain the same. They have been proven effective at hundreds of companies worldwide.

This presents an opportunity to race ahead of the competition. One or more companies in your industry will seize that opportunity, if they haven't already. The rest will be left behind.

So what are you waiting for?

YEAR ONE

First Quarter

Month One

Start with leadership. If the senior leadership team does not believe the organization needs to be transformed, they must be converted. Lay out the case for change using data and information from industry and competitor scans. Explain the possible or likely emergence of serious threats, such as new competitors, disruptive technologies, substitute products, and mega buyers and suppliers. Send the leadership team to observe companies with cultures you wish to emulate and to talk to their leaders. If possible, get them involved in a kaizen event.

Earlier we described how WIKA's Michael Gerster took three of his leaders to a weeklong kaizen event at Hayward Pool Products. The experience energized them and launched WIKA's transformation. Pella's current CEO, along with the vice president of engineering and the CFO, led the company's lean efforts after participating in a kaizen event suggested by one of Pella's board members. "We were coming through a period of time when we were doing significant redesign and new product introductions, and we were struggling," said Mel Haught, who attended that first kaizen event as VP of manufacturing, and who is now the president and CEO. "We were open to ways to make us better."

If data, information, and experience do not open leaders to change, immersing them in the process may. This assumes that the senior leader believes in the need for a transformation and is personally committed to leading it. Lacking such support, your best chance for success is to pilot lean in a business unit or division led by a strong and committed executive, and to use its success to make the case for companywide deployment.

State your direction. Leaders must create a clear, concise, and compelling vision that reinforces the mission and values and focuses on customers, values speed and innovation, demands quality, and recognizes employees as partners in the journey. We provide guidelines in Chapter 3.

Communicate the new course and roadmap. Before you can involve everyone in the transformation, you must communicate the nature of the change, the reasons for the change, the goals of the change, and the role employees will play in making it happen. Leaders must communicate the new positioning relentlessly to employees and other key constituencies. They must communicate personally, honestly, clearly, and frequently.

This is what we mean: Vermeer holds regular leadership meetings for about 200 of the company's leaders, quarterly state-of-the business meetings for all employees, and monthly senior leadership briefings at every plant when the quarterly meeting isn't being held, monthly luncheons with small groups of employees hosted by the CEO, monthly newsletters to all employees and their families, weekly updates in each plant on what's happening in the plants and in certain market segments, and daily start-up meetings in each area to review key metrics. "It's a constant challenge because you can't communicate enough," said Vermeer's president and CEO, Mary Andringa.

Tackle the challenge early by setting up formal and informal ways to communicate with employees. The initial discussions should focus on the coming changes and what it means for employees. Make sure to include opportunities for two-way communication so that leaders can listen and respond to employee concerns.

Assess the current condition. No organization has the resources to work on everything at once. To identify and prioritize the areas you need to improve, assess your current management system. We describe the assessment process in Chapter 3.

Create value stream maps. A high-level value stream map helps you see the major activities taking place in your company to design, produce, and deliver your products and services. It reveals waste, exposes improvement opportunities, and identifies barriers to change. You can then create a future state value stream map to illustrate the direction you want the company to go. You can learn more about the process in Chapter 3.

Plan the first six months. Create a Go Forward Plan to list the actions your organization will take in the first six months to launch the transformation (see Chapter 3 for details). Construct a Cultural Transformation Plan to identify the training and other learning opportunities that will help leaders and other change agents drive the process.

Get the right people in the right jobs. This won't happen in the first month, but the first month is the time to start gathering information and perceptions that will help you assemble a world-class leadership team. We talk about how to do this, including the use of Personalysis profiles, in Chapter 3.

Month Two

Prepare for action. After a month of laying the groundwork for change, you are ready to explain the methodology for rapidly bringing about that change, using the kaizen breakthrough with the entire leadership team. Now is the time to assemble your first kaizen team, introduce team members to the principles of lean, and explain the focus of the first event.

For Heldenfels Enterprises, action included allocating resources to fund the transformation. "We needed to make a dollar commitment to have the discipline to pursue it and to convince our management team and supervisors that this wasn't a fad," said Fred Heldenfels IV, president and CEO. The company's commitment included hiring TBM to guide the process. "We knew we couldn't bootstrap this and read a few books and do it on our own," said Fred.

Organize the workplace. Another action that can help convince people this isn't a fad is called 5S. The 5S method is a process for creating and maintaining an organized, clean, high-performance workplace. It's a conditioning discipline every employee can use to help identify and eliminate non-value-adding activities. The 5S steps (the Japanese word for each step begins with the letter "s") are:

- *Segregate and discard*: Remove what isn't needed.
- *Arrange and identify*: Organize what's left for efficient flow.
- *Clean and inspect daily*: Clean and ensure proper working condition of all equipment.
- *Revisit frequently*: Establish rules for standardizing the new systems and procedures.
- *Motivate to sustain*: Keep everyone involved in sustaining the improvements.

Most companies focus their initial 5S efforts on the same areas where the first kaizen events will be held, but any and all areas can benefit from the process. For Deli Express, its workplace in the field is its trucks. It has held two weeklong 5S events to simplify truck layout, which is now very visual, with photos and prescribed steps.

It also conducted a weeklong 5S event in its office area. "We cleaned out four semis of junk," said President Tom Sween, "and created two conference rooms in the space we saved. It was very powerful. We did a second event to clean up our computer system."

Communicate the next steps. Keep employees informed of the changes underway. "I told people why we are changing, at all levels, to create a sense of urgency," said Michael Gerster, president of WIKA USA. "You've got to say it over and over and over and over again, and then when you think you've said it enough, say it ten more times."

Month Three

Conduct your first kaizen event. "We started our lean journey choosing the best people we had at each plant, and then we went at it full speed. We started doing kaizen events on our main products. That sent a message to the organization that this was not just another flavor of the month," said Hayward's Paul Adelberg. "Our first kaizen events focused on our top priorities, and the results were so compelling that it was an eye-opener. I flew with the president and other executives to each plant to congratulate each team on Friday, when they make their presentations. It let the entire organization know that this was the way we were going to go."

If you choose a visible core process that desperately needs improvement and form a team of your best people to fix it, your first kaizen event will jolt the organization out of business-as-usual mode and demonstrate the value of the new journey. It will also dramatically improve the core process.

Plan your next kaizen event. Target a process. Form a team. Schedule a week. Keep the momentum going.

Remove obstacles. One of the favorite questions the late quality guru W. Edwards Deming asked when he stopped to talk to people during tours of their facilities was, "What gets in the way of your doing your job?" Your old management system generated policies and procedures that may have made sense at one time, but that impede performance now. Process maps and kaizen events reveal these obstacles, as does an organization-wide focus on determining which steps in your processes add value and which should be eliminated.

Communicate early success. Use the formal and informal methods of communication you started establishing in the first month to share the experiences and benefits of the first kaizen event and to keep people informed about what's coming next. The methods of communication include the visible personal involvement of senior leaders, as Paul described at Hayward and Barb King emphasizes at Landscape Structures. "The biggest challenge for us, something we worked very hard at, was frequent, honest, personal communication," she said, "and not just from a front-line supervisor. People see and hear that we're doing great, but it's also leading by example by being on teams and at meetings."

Second Quarter

Month Four

Implement lean principles. The transformational management system values the efficient use of people, equipment, materials, and space. It focuses on improving process capability to get high-quality results in a shorter time at the lowest cost.

The two pillars of this system are one-piece flow and process control. An organization new to these concepts will need expert assistance with understanding and implementing them.

One-piece flow means making and delivering products and services at the rate of customer demand. If customers demand 1,000 widgets for the day, you make 1,000 widgets that day. One-piece flow reduces inventory and other waste, and makes quality defects visible.

The goal of process control is to prevent any type of defect from being passed from one operation in a process to the next. The Japanese term for this is *jidoka*, and many of its elements were developed and/or refined by Toyota including:

- The *5S* method described earlier emphasizes a clean, orderly workplace.
- *Andon* is a visual method of identifying an abnormality in a process and correcting it before more defective products are produced. A blinking red light set off by a defective product is an example. Using *andon*, the first Toyota plant in the U.S. had its assembly line stopped 300 times during its first week of operation. At the end of the week, management held a celebration because employees had found 300 opportunities for improvement.
- *Mistake-proofing* means preventing mistakes from happening. Again, Toyota provides an example. It had a few complaints about squeaks from the hoods of its cars. A study of the hoods revealed that each had thirty-six spot welds, and sometimes a weld was not good, which led to squeaking. Toyota developed a mistake-proofing solution that sent electricity through the welds on a finished hood, illuminating lights for each weld on a visual display. If a light didn't go on it meant the weld was bad and the hood couldn't move until the weld was fixed.
- *Autonomation* involves separating people from the machines they operate by having the machines automatically detect abnormalities, freeing up people to do value-adding work.

- *Set-up time* is the time it takes to change over a piece of equipment from the last piece of one lot to the first good piece of the next, different lot. One of the reasons manufacturers produce large batches of a particular part or product is because it takes so long to switch the equipment from making one part/product to another. One-piece flow opposes batch production, which means reducing set-up time is critical to a smooth flow.

- *Standard work* is a key step during every kaizen event, the point where the new process has been tested and is ready to be documented. "In the first few events, we made big progress on taking inventory out of the system, streamlining the lines, and defining standard work much better," said Pella's Mel Haught. "We took confusion out of the system and put more discipline into the lines."

To sustain kaizen breakthroughs, the new standard work must be documented and posted, or people will revert to what they did before. Standard work helps make process outcomes more predictable. However, standard work is not limited to kaizen events; it is another lean principle that every employee can apply to every process. "Because of our history of licensees, where you had different facilities, structures, and equipment, we had a lot of fragmentation," said Michael Hofmann, senior vice president for Sealy. "We need standardization, so we are driving the discipline of standard work—first and foremost—in every facility, from housekeeping to safety and quality issues."

Some may object that standard work dampens creativity. Landscape Structure's Barb King disagrees. "One of the concerns focusing on standard work was if it would take away from our ability to innovate, but it has embellished it. If you have the foundation in place, you have the latitude and ability to do creative things."

Continue kaizen events. Involving more people in these events, including all senior leaders, helps institutionalize the culture changes. "The old mentality has always been, 'Let's have twenty one-hour meetings every week,' and it would take months to get somewhere," said Scott

Mitchell, senior vice president of business improvement for First Data. "Now we see people doing kaizen events regularly. We see people document on the wall what their process is. They talk about value-added versus non-value-added and what it means to customers. But it's hard to escape the past."

Communicate the culture change. Amana set up a "War Room" where functional leaders meet with the vice president of operations for fifteen minutes every morning to review key metrics. Safety, quality, cost, delivery, and kaizen data are displayed on the room's walls for six assembly lines, four other areas, and the entire plant.

The Amana displays are a variation of SQCD (Safety, Quality, Cost, Delivery) charts, an example of which is shown in Figure 8-1. The charts show performance on the key strategic and operational measures for the organization, which are ultimately linked to policy deployment (see Chapter 4).

Figure 8-1   Example of SQCD Chart

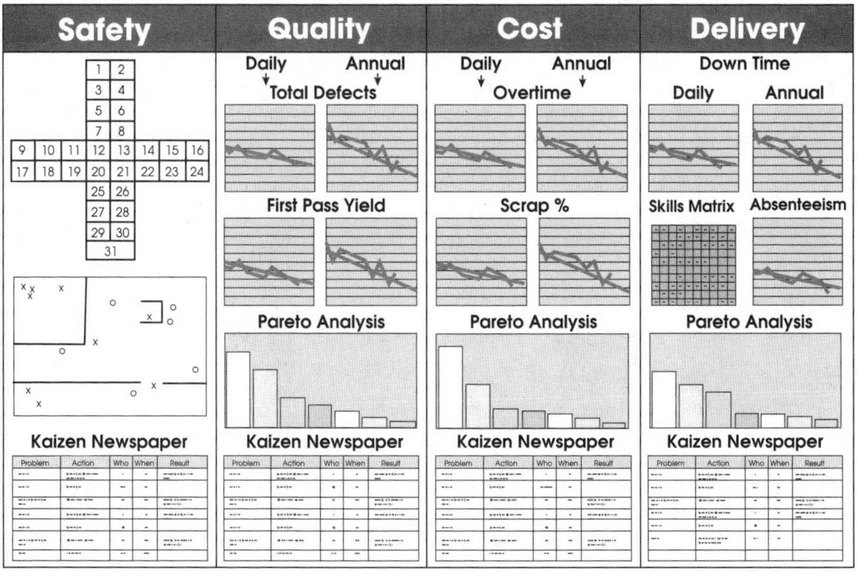

Months Five and Six

Continue holding kaizen events, implementing lean principles, and communicating progress on the transformation. After a few months, you start wondering when the new management model will replace the old. Well, it probably took decades to get the old system to where it is today, and it will take years for the culture to embrace the new one.

"We haven't cracked the code yet," said Tom Sween of Deli Express, which is now well into the third year of its lean journey. "The kaizen approach is great, you can stop the bus and get everyone involved and make changes, but then Monday comes and people snap back to their old habits. We're still figuring out how to sustain the changes."

Stay the course.

Third and Fourth Quarters

The top priority for the second half of the first year is sustaining the steps you have taken. Most organizations have their hands full changing the culture, and our intent here is not to make that task any harder by adding more things to do. However, a lean transformation includes other elements critical to long-term success. We present these elements in the remainder of this chapter for you to consider when the timing is right for your company.

Align through policy deployment. Use policy deployment to build consensus on the critical activities that will generate growth and long-term success, and to align everyone with those priorities. We describe the policy deployment process in Chapter 4.

Develop supplier partnerships. Begin by communicating your lean journey to your key suppliers. Suppliers are used to their customers demanding lower prices, and they're tired of it. If, on the other hand, you use your new lean experiences to help your suppliers reduce their costs and inventory, you will strengthen your partnership. And if they decide to take the same journey, you will have a stronger and more efficient ally able to deliver fair and competitive prices.

A typical supplier launch model begins with a briefing for a few of your most important suppliers, along with the suppliers' participation in kaizen events for a process that the suppliers influence. In the second month, a joint logistics event is held with the suppliers. A site assessment in the third month initiates the lean transformation, and the suppliers start holding kaizen events in the fourth month.

Pella followed a similar approach with a key supplier of glass, its second highest commodity in terms of dollars spent. Through the supplier kaizen approach, the supplier, Cardinal Glass Industries, reduced setups to improve production flexibility and eliminated unnecessary paperwork and packaging. It ships glass in returnable "harps," produces glass to Pella's line sequence, and delivers it twice daily to the assembly lines. Pella's glass inventory has shrunk from seventeen days to six hours, which has saved 25,000 square feet of floor space. Scheduling has gone from weekly batches to line sequence. Glass breakage and scrap has declined from 3 percent to 0.3 percent.

Sustain the change. Several of the activities we've listed help institutionalize the cultural transformation, including senior leadership involvement, kaizen events, policy deployment, and communication. We also suggest the early creation of a kaizen promotion office to align projects with your business objectives, promote the process, manage the projects, sustain the gains, and build an internal team of experts. The ideal candidate to lead this office is passionate about the changes underway, has earned the respect of the organization by participating in kaizen events and establishing himself or herself as an effective change agent, and has the ear of senior leaders (or is a senior leader). Technical qualifications are not important; they can be learned.

YEAR TWO

During the first three years of the transformation, you will lower the water and expose a lot of rocks. Streamline a process and you discover that your equipment isn't as reliable as it needs to be. Move toward one-piece flow only to find out that your suppliers are holding you back. Get suppliers on track and you learn that demand—how customers buy—isn't what it should be. Each improvement exposes more areas to address.

"When I first started practicing kaizen, I talked to someone who had been doing it for five years," said Hayward's Paul Adelberg. "I asked him how far his company had come. He said that after the first year he thought they were 80 percent there, and after five years he thought they were 20 percent there. We're six years into this and we're not 20 percent there yet. It's a never-ending journey that teaches you not be become complacent."

It's important to remember that this journey has no finish line. There's a danger in trying to do too much so fast that you can't sustain the gains. Our mantra is narrow and deep. Tackle the rocks you expose and don't worry yet about the ones you can't see. Prioritize the opportunities and start at the top of the list. Narrow and deep.

Review performance. One key to sustaining both the energy of the transformation and the gains it produces is reviewing performance. In Chapter 4 we recommended that senior leaders review performance on policy deployment projects every month. The policy deployment matrix (see Chapter 4) calls for measures of performance on key projects and identifies project owners. The owners update senior management on progress during the monthly reviews.

One problem we frequently encounter with these reviews is senior management's willingness to let sub-par performance slide. Leaders live with the issues being addressed through policy deployment. On a daily basis, those issues compete with many others for attention and resources. Leaders know that everything can't get done, that priorities shift, that it can take longer to complete a task than planned. When a policy deployment project fails to meet expectations, it is often too easy for the owner to convince his or her peers that the problem is being addressed, but it will take longer to solve and, as a result, the project may not meet its goals.

We take away that crutch. We found that when TBM started facilitating quarterly reviews, the success rate of a company's policy deployment process improved dramatically. The reason outside assistance is effective is because we are able to confront project owners, remind them of why completing the project according to plan is necessary, ignore the excuses, and demand countermeasures and accountability. If a problem exists, the solution is not to accept it, but to solve it. We ask what countermeasures the owner has instituted to get the project back on track. At the next quarterly review, we discuss how well the countermeasures worked and what others might be necessary. In this way, we help build a performance culture that values innovation, accountability, and results.

We also recommend a two-day planning and review meeting every six months to talk about what's working and what isn't, alignment, objectives, resources, internal and external changes, and sustaining improvements. We engage senior leaders in visualizing what the next six months should look like and in connecting upcoming kaizen events to policy deployment and longer-term strategies.

Improve business processes. The lean transformation gains broad traction when you begin holding kaizen breakthrough events for your business processes. A business process is any repetitive, transactional process that does *not* produce your products or services, such as human resource processes (recruiting, training, administering benefits, etc.), financial processes (closing, accounts payable/receivable, budgeting, etc.), production planning and scheduling, procurement, product/service design, legal/regulatory compliance, marketing, and sales.

The first step in improving these processes is to identify and prioritize them. Each department or unit must list what it does in terms of processes. For each process, the department or unit needs to determine how long the process takes in terms of work content and lead time, how often employees perform the process, and who is involved. Senior leaders collect and analyze this information to assess the effectiveness and efficiency of each process, and to rank them for kaizen events.

WIKA divides its kaizen activities into production improvements and business process improvements. Every project has a sponsor from senior management to show management's commitment, and to help sustain it.

Kodak turned its attention to business processes in 2003. "We've had an enormous amount of improvements in human resources, non-manufacturing units, and in the business units themselves in sales, marketing, and the back office," said Charles Barrentine, who directs Kodak's business process improvement effort. "We still have a long way to go, but we've been saving tens of millions of dollar a month."

Heldenfels Enterprises initiated business process kaizens in 2004 in accounting and financial areas, and in contract administration. "The more measurable and easily grasped, the more successful you are," said Fred Heldenfels. "The simpler the process you are trying to improve, the quicker and more measurable the results. Our goal is for every department to have clear, simple performance metrics, and to engage in business process kaizens to improve how they score on those metrics."

With the addition of business process kaizen events, companies must find the right balance between production and non-production events. Deli Express held more than 100 kaizen events in the first three years of its lean journey. It runs at least one production and one business process kaizen every month. For Jason Incorporated, four out of five kaizen events focus on manufacturing, but President and CEO David Westgate sees the value of improving business processes. "We've had several business process kaizens focused on the product development, scheduling, and order entry. Historically, I've found as much opportunity in business processes as in manufacturing."

As we noted in Chapter 1, Western Union refers to its kaizen events as "million dollar projects." Each project targets a business process.

Promote daily improvement. Institutionalizing the lean transformation ultimately means involving everyone in the process every day. Our formal approach to this is called Managing for Daily Improvement (MDI). It starts with training on identifying and addressing areas to improve. Those who receive the training are then responsible for delivering results.

After training managers in MDI, Pella created a formal program in which each manager devotes between one and three hours per day to MDI activities concentrated in one particular area—standard work, visual management, 5S, etc. The manager reports out at the end of the cycle, which could be a month. Each department manager owes the company 2,000 hours in savings every year from his/her MDI efforts.

Landscape Structures extended MDI training to all employees. Employees then decide which continuous improvement projects to work on in their areas. People come up with ideas and discuss them with their managers. They know the criteria for projects, the standard format for what to look for, and how they will report out. Project length varies from completion within a month to projects that take several months. Reports on MDI projects are made every day at 4 p.m. A weekly intranet calendar identifies who is reporting each day. Anyone can go to the meetings, with senior management attending as many as possible.

"There are two very great aspects of this that I didn't expect," said Barb King. "One is the complete 'we-can-do-it' attitude that our company has. There's so much pride and understanding of how important our processes are through kaizen events and MDI.

"The other part is, because of the involvement of people in kaizen and MDIs, it has given people a real chance to develop in terms of presenting in front of employees. As a manager, it gives you the opportunity to see in depth all of the people in the company."

Discover the Voice of the Customer. Start simple: Decide in which customer group or market segment you want to increase your market share. Identify the "real customers" in that group, the people who buy and use your product or service. Assemble a cross-functional team to learn the Voice of the Customer for that customer group or market segment. Follow the process outlined in Chapter 5.

Dedicating time to visiting customers often stirs up resistance among those who believe they already know what customers' want. Too often, their perception is not shared by your customers. "A lot of companies today are still focused inside out," said WIKA's Michael Gerster. "You've got to be in front of customers to find out what you can do for them. Think of being in the customers' shoes. Shape your organization and products and services so that customers perceive that you are meeting their expectations."

Companies that pride themselves on being close to their customers typically need to take the next step of formally listening and observing to uncover stated and unarticulated needs. "We've always been a flat organization, and we've always been out with our customers," said Barb King of Landscape Structures. "The difference has been in understanding and living our premier provider position in terms of what we want to look like with the customer and what is of value to them."

Improve the product design process. As we noted in Chapter 6, survival depends more and more on accelerating the process of developing new products that meet customers' expectations and getting them to market faster, with higher quality and lower cost. Chapter 6 describes how you can do this.

Develop Six Sigma Process capability. As with implementing lean principles, you will need experienced people to train Black Belts and Green Belts and to implement LeanSigma. We recommend developing Six Sigma capability after six to eighteen months of solid sustainment of basic lean methodologies and robust adherence to standard work.

Link to actual customer demand. Lean distribution is the third order of business after getting your house in order and involving key suppliers in the transformation. By linking directly to customer demand, you can increase your flexibility, eliminate waste, improve speed, lower costs, and improve customer satisfaction.

The goal is to create "pull" by the end customer on your production process, which supports one-piece flow and helps reduce inventory. Applica Consumer Products provides an example. With its line of Black & Decker labeled products, Applica is the market leader in several small appliance categories such as toaster ovens and irons. It began its lean journey in 1994. By 1998, it had cut overall inventories by nearly 70 percent in its manufacturing plants. Defect levels at 20,000 parts per million had been slashed to 200 ppm (and are now approaching zero defects or Six Sigma-level quality). Yet despite its operational efficiency, Applica suffered from too much inventory in the demand chain, and had to resort to fire sales and the all-out price wars that racked the small appliance industry.

President and COO Harry Schulman knew that cost-cutting was a dead-end strategy. His team looked at the distribution chain and saw a different race they could run. "We can help our retailers cut inventory 75 percent and eliminate forecasting, sell-ins, and markdown sales, while our competitors still make them jump through those hoops," said Harry. "No more guessing. We can get new, innovative products to market more quickly—and that boosts the image of both the maker and the store. None of our competitors can do that."

Working with retailers, Applica removed more than $80 million in finished goods inventory from its own pipeline. It now replenishes products based on its customers' point-of-sale in four weeks or less, compared to sixteen weeks or more for its competitors. "Now it's not about price," said Harry. "It's a business partnership."

Evolve accounting to align with the new management model. Standard cost accounting and the transformational management system don't mix. It and other such accounting practices are good at hiding inventory expense, often making it look like a good thing. However, we know that excess inventory is just dead weight that hinders your ability to be responsive, which means you need a better accounting system that promotes simplicity and openness, a new way of categorizing costs by value stream, rather than by department, and better communication of the financial gains being made. TBM describes the new lean accounting system in *Real Numbers*, which was published in 2002.

Stay the course. By the end of the first year, much of the new energy around the transformation has dissipated. The "low-hanging fruit" has been picked, and what remains is harder to find and harder to reach. The role of senior leaders changes from spearheading a new initiative to sustaining it, but the means of doing both remain the same. Participate in kaizen events. Talk to customers. Listen to employees. Review performance and implement countermeasures to stay on track. And communicate your company's vision and values, strategies, goals, progress, and expectations.

YEAR THREE AND BEYOND

The success of the new transformational management system lies in a company's ability to sustain its lean journey. Issues with sustaining the transformation typically appear during the third year and are caused by two very different problems: apathy or speed.

Apathy settles in when senior leaders decide to turn their attention to other matters in the mistaken belief that the lean transformation is self-sustaining. No organizational change is self-sustaining. Cultural change requires an ongoing, visible commitment by senior leaders evident in their daily leadership, constant communication, and personal involvement. Delegating this responsibility sends a clear message that other things are now more important.

Speed can derail the journey when a company moves too fast to sustain the gains. People need time and opportunity to learn and practice their new skills. Standard work must be documented, communicated, and followed. Managers and supervisors must adapt to doing less firefighting and more enabling and enforcing standard work. Redesigned processes need time for the kinks to be smoothed out and flow to be established. Relevant measures must be identified and tracked to stay focused on the results of improvements. Rushing from one project to the next without sustaining the gains only wears people out.

While it's tempting to hurry up and eliminate waste and get closer to customers and transform how you do business—and early success feeds that desire—you need to secure the improvements as you go. "Our biggest struggle has been sustaining what comes out of events, and accountability," said Pat Alexander, president and CEO of Cold Spring Granite. "We found out what we thought we were getting out of events wasn't long-term. We had to reevaluate, and it comes down to accountability. We haven't held people accountable very well. Now we're basically making contracts with leaders and managers, up front, on goals and new initiatives. I think people are slowly starting to understand that we're serious about this."

Leverage lean for growth. Phase III of the lean transformation targets strategies for growth. During the first three years of the journey, you are creating greater flexibility, more capacity, and a stronger focus on customer needs. You are now positioned to go after opportunities in the marketplace that you couldn't pursue before.

In the previous chapter, we described how companies use value innovation to run a different race. Some of our clients decide to use their financial gains to fund their acquisition strategies. Hayward Pool Products bought two companies and moved their operations into 35,000 square feet of space freed up by lean projects. We mentioned how Jason Incorporated places a "Reserved for New Business" sign in front of empty work areas opened up by lean projects. "We're looking at leveraging our lean accomplishments in the marketplace to make new acquisitions," said Jason's David Westgate. "That's the reward of becoming lean."

Begin conducting point kaizens. After two or three years of practicing weeklong kaizens, a company can graduate to conducting point kaizens, which are one-, two-, or three-day kaizen events focused on simpler issues or projects with a narrow focus. Point kaizen teams may be as small as two to four people, with team members that have participated in weeklong events.

Good candidates for a point kaizen include:

- A bottleneck exists in production.
- A quality issue persists in spite of individual efforts to resolve it.
- A particular operation has a high defect rate.
- A need for standard work is evident at a particular workstation.
- A narrowly focused issue exists that has a severely negative impact on flow.
- An item on a thirty-day list from a previous kaizen week remains unresolved or incomplete.

At the beginning of 2005, Heldenfels Enterprises decided to conduct a kaizen event on improving safety. It conducted a point kaizen to identify the major safety hazards, producing a Pareto chart that identified and prioritized the most common safety incidents. "We took that information into a full week kaizen and came out with several projects that we've been implementing since January," said Fred Heldenfels. "Our focus was to cut into our incident rate, and we're beginning to see the results of that."

In the end, sustaining the transformation and maintaining the potency of the antidote requires a constant emphasis on the fundamentals, the "blocking and tackling" that produce and secure the gains. The next chapter addresses how your company can get back to the basics to ensure long-term success.

CHAPTER NINE

Sustaining the Journey

Few issues vex the leaders of successful companies more
than how to sustain their gains. While a "burning platform" may
compel people to jump, once the fire is doused, they have no
problem abandoning their new environment and climbing back
onto that old deck. Many a leader has rationalized starting new
fires—or creating imaginary ones—to keep people from yearn-
ing for a return to the "good old days." The fact that they weren't
that good has little impact on the longing to go back.

We differ from a lot of companies and consultants that see lean as a short-
term solution to immediate problems. They, too, want to eliminate waste,
but the eliminating includes laying off people who are no longer needed in
their streamlined processes. They, too, want to cut costs, but cost-cutting
means requiring people to do more, not just to work more efficiently, breed-
ing stress and dissent. Their version of lean is destructive, not transformative, trading off short-term gains for long-term distrust, pinning the hope
for survival on shrinking rather than growing.

Because we've seen the rebirth of companies that have spent years institutionalizing their transformational management systems, we understand the value of this long-term journey. Just look at Toyota. The question is, how does a company sustain its new way of operating once the initial buzz is gone? How do you keep accelerating processes and removing waste and improving quality when tempted to relax and enjoy? At what point can you, as a leader, turn your attention to other things?

"I don't think it's getting burned out, but you lose the essence of why you do this," said Mel Haught, president and CEO of Pella, which started its lean journey in 1993. "That's the biggest risk for me. I don't think you can ever relax or assume that you've got it."

At Landscape Structures, the stages of the transformation help sustain it. "We've moved from one stage to another, first in manufacturing and now in internal office functions," said Barb King. "Those pose different challenges. The third stage will be external to suppliers and representatives. We know we've got these different stages and that helps keep us focused so it doesn't get stale. Unless we create a burning platform, I don't think we can expect to have that initial adrenaline rush we got the first time. Now our challenge is to keep it exciting."

To hold onto their hard-earned competitive advantage, companies like Pella and Landscape Structures must embed the processes that got them there: internalizing the Voice of the Customer, nurturing innovation, improving operational effectiveness, extending lean to the entire value chain, and strengthening their strategic positions. They cannot stand still. As Will Rogers said, "Even if you're on the right track, you'll get run over if you just sit there."

In our experience, we've found that the best way to secure gains and move forward is to get back to the antidote's basics. We describe "the basics" as the Five Rs:

- *Responsiveness* to key customer needs
- *Reliability* to deliver quality solutions on time
- *Rhythm* to match output to customer demands

- *Responsibility* to all stakeholders to use resources wisely
- *Relevance* to adapt to changing customer needs through innovation

RESPONSIVENESS

Not only do customers' needs change, but your understanding of those needs also changes. Your early Voice of the Customer activities helped you identify and prioritize key requirements. They may have exposed unarticulated needs to add to the list. That list can grow like a child's birthday wish list if you don't have some way of filtering the items to sift out the less important. Earlier we described how Southwest Airlines and Hotel Formule1 revolutionized their industries by choosing *not* to provide what everyone thought were essential services. As your Voice of the Customer efforts mature, you will need to develop criteria you can apply to each customer need to decide if you want to create, eliminate, raise, or reduce your response to that need.

At the same time, customers' expectations will rise as you satisfy their needs. What was once considered leading edge will become standard practice and new levels of performance will be required. Differentiating your company means setting the bar higher every year compared to a dynamic benchmark. If the best in your business is achieving higher performance levels than you are, determine what those levels are and how they compare to your performance, and then set goals to not only close the gap, but to become industry best.

If you are already industry best, compare performance to world-class companies outside your industry and target their performance levels. If you're among the best in that group as well, compare your performance to yourself. We encourage clients in this position to strive for a 10 to 15 percent annual improvement in productivity, and a 50 percent reduction in quality defects. Some leaders balk at such aggressive goals, but we've seen companies achieve much harder ones. For example, when Bob Galvin led Motorola in the 1980s and early '90s, his mantra was "10x": a ten times improvement in quality year to year. Now *that's* an aggressive goal.

Staying aggressive is one way to sustain the transformation. It also happens to be critical to your long-term success. Recently, *Business Week* published an article about the Indian business-process outsourcing industry, which grew 40 percent to $5.8 billion in 2004 and is expected to grow ten times that by 2012. The article focused on Wipro, a company in Bangalore that has 42,000 employees and $1.7 billion in revenues. Wipro sent a bunch of managers to Toyota to learn how it does lean manufacturing. When they came back, Wipro asked them how it could run an outsourcing operation the Toyota way, putting people together to eliminate waste and create process flow. Within a couple of years Wipro had used lean concepts to improve productivity by 43 percent and reduce rework (waste) from 18 percent to 2 percent.

For business leaders in the U.S., it's frightening to think about competing with foreign companies that are dramatically improving quality and reducing costs, while paying employees a fraction of the wages Americans earn. "You can see the effects of outsourcing in the furniture and textile industries everywhere," said Michael Hofmann, senior vice president at Sealy. "In this region of North Carolina, we've lost 24,300 jobs since 2000."

To compete in this changing arena, Sealy decided to turn "Made in the USA" into an advantage. "Staying local is really about producing great products close to the customer," said Hofmann. "More than 85 percent of our customers are within 300 miles of one of our facilities. Since we're shipping products that are mostly air, and we deliver all orders in days versus months, it's a significant factor in our cost structure that we remain close to our customer base. These issues mandate that we have regional and small facilities that operate by lean manufacturing principles."

Asian manufacturers quote eight- to ten-week lead times, which puts pressure on them to forecast accurately to produce the right mix of products and manage their inventory. It also means they have significant investments in working capital. Sealy's plants make products to order within forty-eight to seventy-two hours. "Keeping our production in the U.S. isn't patriotic, it's fundamental to our business strategy. Our strategy is to compete on innovation, customization, and responsiveness," said Hofmann.

For lean companies, getting back to basics means being responsive to ever-changing customer needs. And one of the key characteristics of responsiveness is speed.

RELIABILITY

Responsiveness is a key component of every organization's prime directive: getting the right things to the right people at the right time. What's right is determined by the next person in the process and, ultimately, by your customers. And that brings us to the second component of the directive: how *reliably* you deliver the right things to the right people at the right time.

The biggest issue we find with reliability is consistency. Those companies that value standard work, follow predictable processes, measure reliability, and improve on those measures to achieve consistent levels of performance upon which their customers and partners can depend.

"Our ability to significantly reduce lead times and improve reliability was a big deal for Pella and, ultimately, a tremendous benefit for our customers," said Mel Haught. "We took a 40 to 60 percent reduction in lead times and drove reliability from the 80 percent range to 98-plus percent. That made us much more reliable to our channel partners so they could quote windows and doors more reliably to their customers. Once our Pella Window and Door Stores could trust us to ship what we said we could ship, they could reduce their inventory. We were much more competitive."

Sajjan Agarwal credits his company's focus on responsiveness and reliability for its ability to grow 250 percent since 2000. Sajjan is the CEO of Sigma Electric Manufacturing Company. Headquartered in Raleigh, North Carolina, Sigma manufactures more than 1,500 standard products for the electrical device industry (conduit fittings, cable connectors and fasteners, etc.) and power transmission and distribution industries (transformer connectors and power line hardware), as well as custom solutions for a variety of industries.

Sigma is a global solutions provider. It has four manufacturing facilities in India that offer international customers product design, tool design, project management, production engineering, manufacturing, packaging solutions, and supply chain management, with world-class performance through lean and Six Sigma, and communications through advanced technology. All sales and customer support, private label packaging, and central distribution take place in Raleigh.

"Ten years ago, Sigma was a smaller operation," said Sajjan. "Before the Internet, my knowledge of and relationships with customers were very important. That knowledge suddenly became deliverable to everyone. What do I do? We're in a commodity-type market. When companies start to look outside, to outsource, what is it they want? Two things became very important: reliability and responsiveness."

To meet these needs, Sajjan invested heavily in infrastructure, in equipment, training, and communication. "During the late 1990s to 2001, people suddenly started going to China, India, and Mexico to outsource, and they saw our model and we started getting a lot of business," Sajjan said. "I was having trouble managing it, and then I found lean. I've been in the United States for thirty years and I had to throw out everything I had learned, like batch manufacturing. In the past, when I sat with my people to solve a problem, it was always automation or something else that cost a lot. My thought process was, 'We need to grow, so we need a new facility and new machines.' Today, it's creativity before capital. You can do a lot more with the same things."

While Sigma's dramatic growth came from leveraging lean to become a solutions provider, the foundation for that growth is reliability and responsiveness. Neither can be taken for granted. A problem we frequently encounter in companies that have been on this journey for a few years is that they become complacent. Their measurement and feedback systems have atrophied from lack of use, and reliability and responsiveness have suffered. Managers who have been waiting for an excuse to trash lean pounce on declining performance as a sign that the lean transformation has run its course, as if lean principles suddenly no longer apply. Worsening results are not a failure of the system; they are a failure of management.

Sealy has a manufacturing facility in Chicago that consistently delivers world-class results. At 10:30 a.m. every day, the plant's leaders and managers visit every section of the facility. The head of each section uses the area's performance board to explain what they have done to improve performance over the previous day, what one area they are targeting to improve (such as 5S, safety, delivery), where they are, and where they're going to be. The entire tour takes thirty minutes, and the sense of urgency and ownership it creates is unbelievable.

That's what we mean by consistency.

RHYTHM

Applying lean principles to a process reduces waste and improves flow. The goal of one-piece flow is to make something when a customer demands it, thus eliminating inventory. Dell provides an excellent example, sending customer orders to the manufacturing floor at the beginning of the day and then assembling computers that fill those orders—and not building a single one that hasn't been requested.

The lean term for precisely matching production to customer demand is takt time. Takt is a German word for the baton a conductor uses to control the timing or rhythm of an orchestra. For a business, takt time is your sell rate.

You compute takt time by dividing the net operating time per period (say, an eight-hour shift) by the customer requirements for that period. Let's say a shift is 450 minutes once you subtract breaks and cleanup time. Customers require 9,000 units a month. With twenty working days in the month, each shift must produce 450 units. Thus, the takt time is sixty seconds. They must make one unit every sixty seconds to meet customer demand.

Since customer demand fluctuates, we recommend a systematic monthly planning process to establish optimal flow. During the first two weeks of the month, you gather information from the marketplace and analyze it to look for short-term trends. You then meet to decide if the current takt time needs to be adjusted and, if so, to what new standard. Once agreement is reached, a contract states the takt time for the next four weeks and everyone sticks to that contract—although they have the freedom to change the mix of units being produced.

This freedom is essential to maintaining rhythm with your customers. We know that abnormalities occur. You need to institute the discipline of pull to react to them in a system designed to operate on takt time rhythm. A lean expert from Toyota, Yoshiki Iwata, once told Anand that creating the discipline of pull from the customer in a production system is like the impulse reaction of your hand while you grab a hot cup of coffee: Even if you have an orderly nervous system that sends out immediate signals to your brain, and there's a response from the brain to move your hand away, you don't wait for that signal. You automatically move your hand because it's a normal reaction to an abnormal situation. In the same way, work cells must be able to respond to abnormal demand without waiting for a signal from the central system.

The ability to be in rhythm with customers evolves as one-piece flow precisely at the takt time becomes part of a company's DNA. It synchronizes at the macro level with the monthly schedule. At the micro level, the work-cell produces the daily mix based on actual customer demands. This is accomplished with continuous reduction in changeover time and consistent adherence to standard work. It applies to service companies and to business processes as well. In fact, through our work with call centers and other service processes, we've seen seasonal variations, as well as differences in demand by day of the week and hour of the day. As one-piece flow becomes embedded in a service company's DNA, work groups will become adept at varying staffing levels and adjusting flow to match the rhythms of customer demand.

RESPONSIBILITY

Senior leaders have a fiduciary responsibility to make sure they are conserving and leveraging their organizations' financial, physical, intellectual, and human capital. They must do more with less. Throughout this book, we've described how the lean journey helps leaders do more with less:

- Landscape Structures freed up 35,000 square feet of space in its first year.
- Western Union saves roughly $1 million with every kaizen project.
- Deli Express has shown double-digit growth every year since it started its journey.

- The Iowa DNR reduced the time to get a new source construction permit from sixty-two days to six days and eliminated a backlog of 600 applications.
- Hayward Pool Products gained ten market share points and doubled its business with no change in direct labor headcount.
- Not only did Hayward not have to build a planned $8 million facility to accommodate its growth, it closed a 240,000-square-foot plant by creating space for its activities in two other plants.
- Pella has quadrupled its window and door sales since embarking on its lean journey in 1993, a rate significantly better than that of its primary competitor.
- La Cage aux Sports tripled its value in five years.
- Ventana Medical Systems grows 20 to 25 percent per year with a significantly smaller increase in total headcount.
- A year after emerging from bankruptcy, Special Metals Wiggin had reduced inventory by 24 percent and doubled profitability.
- From 2001 to 2004, Hubbell grew net sales by 54 percent, net income by 320 percent, and sales per employee by 17 percent, while reducing inventory by 53 percent and space by more than 1.5 million square feet.
- Working with retailers, Applica Consumer Products removed more than $80 million in finished goods inventory.
- Vermeer reduced work-in-process by 55 percent while increasing production productivity by 26 percent.
- WIKA USA planned on 5 percent growth in 2004, but realized better than 20 percent.
- From 2001 to early 2005, Amana reduced in-plant defects by 38 percent and improved sales per employee by 60 percent.
- Sealy improved overall factory productivity by 19 percent in twelve months.
- By implementing one-piece flow, Jason Incorporated reduced capital spending by $5 million, inventory levels by $8 million, and floor space by 300,000 square feet.
- Kodak saves tens of millions of dollars every month through lean business processes.

In our experience, capital investments also go down by half in the first two to four years of a company's lean journey. When companies are ready to leverage lean for growth, they do not reinvest in the monuments of the past, but in simple and inexpensive machines and capabilities that deliver the flexibility and responsiveness they need.

This is also the point when leaders must address their organization's natural tendency to rest on its laurels. Most of the savings in the first year come from "low-hanging fruit," from the obvious inefficiencies that are easy to spot and relatively easy to fix. As that fruit is plucked, however, and the remaining problems are hidden deeper in the process, people often decide they've done enough.

In the third year of its journey, one of our clients with multiple business units faced such resistance. All the general managers announced that they had done enough in inventory reduction and had reached the point where they could do no more. We asked them to look at the excess inventory that was over their own current inventory policy and they discovered that they were nearly $90 million over policy. The CEO told the general managers not to do anything that year to reduce inventory except to take the amount over policy down to $30 million.

The best way to overcome resistance to continuous improvement is to present the facts. In this client's case, two facts helped melt away the general managers' resistance: the company was still nearly $90 million over the target they had set, and they still had a large inventory of raw materials. The facts indicated that further reductions were both necessary and possible.

In the last chapter, we quoted Hayward's Paul Adelberg, who said his company is six years into the lean transformation and it's not even 20 percent there yet. It is senior leadership's responsibility to understand the never-ending nature of the lean journey, to communicate the changes yet to be made, and to hold people accountable for improving performance. The old system provides logical and natural excuses for failing to perform. It offers places to hide. Senior leaders need to present the facts that show the need for change and hold people accountable for acting on those facts, because in the end, senior leaders have a fiduciary responsibility to do more with less.

Resistance to unending improvement is not the only symptom of a stalled journey. Other signs include:

- Key leaders who were lean disciples leaving the company
- New visionary leaders not on board
- Customers saying you're not as responsive as you were
- Suppliers noting that you're not as demanding as you used to be
- People ignoring key metrics or how you're performing on them
- Inventory waste creeping back in
- Standard work not being followed
- The need to customize your approach
- Complacency

Senior leaders must be aware of signals that momentum may have slowed and act quickly to get things back on track. That means instilling a sense of urgency by bringing the brutal reality of the marketplace to the people, and holding them accountable for results. It means diligently communicating the financial, quality, delivery, and customer impact of the changes you've already made. And it means strengthening the connections with your customers to bring their perspective into your decision-making by listening to the Voice of the Customer.

Leaders should use the discipline of policy deployment to help fulfill their responsibility to improve and grow. Consistently look for things that are not going as planned to catch them as early as possible. Help your organization learn to celebrate an early request for help or the early deployment of countermeasures.

RELEVANCE

The growth of the global marketplace has made it harder for companies to stay relevant doing the same things for any length of time. When you listen to customers, you become aware that their needs are changing, and changing faster. You realize that they now have ever quicker access to more universal sources of supply. To remain relevant, you must constantly reinvent the products and services you offer, and that means staying close to your customers and involving your whole organization in value innovation focused on customer needs.

This is no small task. WIKA, for example, faces the challenge of cultural and language issues arising from having employees from thirty-two different countries under the same roof. "I would like learning and innovation to be faster," said Michael Gerster. "The entire activity is still on the shoulders of a handful of people instead of migrating to every level where it's much more dynamic, more efficient, and faster. Still, too many of our employees come here to pick up their paychecks and go home. It's very difficult to change that attitude if you can't reach them through the cultural and language barriers."

The larger and more global the company, the longer the transformation will take—but it *will* take. As more and more employees participate in kaizen events, they will bring the passion for improving performance back to their work groups and departments, and infect coworkers with their enthusiasm. At Hayward, nearly 80 percent of employees have participated in kaizen events, some in as many as fifteen events. They value the experience so much, they want to do it all the time. Vermeer has had 70 percent participation, and the *average* number of events per participant is eight. Pella conducted a cultural survey in 2002 that showed a 13.5 percent higher job satisfaction rating among employees who had been on a kaizen team in the past twelve months. It turns out, the best way to involve employees in the transformation, to get them to care about customer needs and operational effectiveness and innovation, is to actually *involve* them through kaizen events and other approaches we've described in this book, such as point kaizens and Managing for Daily Improvement.

Involving employees in value innovation focused on customer needs requires a profound knowledge of those needs. We've seen few better examples of how to acquire, communicate, and act on that knowledge than Vermeer's market-based strategy.

Vermeer launched this strategy in the summer of 2004. It began with determining who its customers are and what their needs are through face-to-face interviews, phone interviews, Internet research, and on-site observation. The people gathering the information focused on end customers to understand their markets, the factors of competition, what priority they place on those factors, and where the gaps are. They looked for strategic opportunities in the factors their customers valued that nobody was providing.

They captured all of this information electronically and organized it around customer segments. Vermeer used the information to develop value innovation curves, such as those we presented in Chapter 7 for Southwest Airlines and Hotel Formule1. It currently has fourteen different value innovation curves with more markets yet to address. It continues to populate the value innovation curves with the knowledge gained through ongoing customer contact. "I can go online now and look at a value innovation curve and see how many contacts are in that database, the key factors, and competitors and how they rate," said Mary Andringa, Vermeer's president and CEO. "I can click on a tab where I can enter an unstructured discussion with a customer and that automatically goes into queue and we analyze it and everything is tied back. That's how we summarize the data."

With data in hand, Vermeer identifies a solution based on the value innovation curve. "We created a five-step approach to creating a value proposition," said Glenda Vander Wilt, continuous improvement manager of market-based strategy at Vermeer. "We ensure that the value proposition will be sustainable and will differentiate us. We develop a financial analysis, the facts we want to communicate to customers. We develop a story for how we are going to sell this to customers, what words we want to use. The last step is communication."

Despite the early success of its market-based strategy, Vermeer still faces challenges. It has to get people to use the process. It's working to train its sales people to sell total solutions, which is a change in mindset from selling specific products. The challenge is to remain relevant to its customers, build loyalty, and increase market share.

"Over the last seven years, one of our overriding strategies has been implementing lean," said Mary. "A partner with lean is market-based strategy. Now it's about implementing it into our culture and into the whole value stream, to suppliers and distribution channels. It's broad, but also strategic, so they are like ten-year plans that we keep modifying and improving on."

By focusing every stage of the lean journey and every employee on customer needs, a company remains relevant to its customers, and the ongoing transformation remains relevant to the success of the organization.

SUSTAINING THE JOURNEY

Every organization faces a moment of truth for a new initiative. Most of the time in most companies, complacency sets in and the initiative fades away. The fact that nearly everyone has witnessed this explains the biggest threat to any lean transformation—that people will hunker down and do the minimum necessary because they know that this, too, will pass, and if they wait it out, they can return to business as usual. Too often, this is exactly what happens.

Leaders can choose another option. They must believe that the lean journey is their company's key to survival and growth, and they must be committed to guiding people on that journey. They must be aware of the signs of complacency, anticipate them, and neutralize them. They must keep people focused on the basics of the antidote, on the Five Rs that ensure continuous improvement in meeting customer needs. They must nurture a work environment that involves all employees in improving, participating, and innovating. They must communicate customer needs and competitive challenges, strategies and plans, and failures and successes. Over and over and over.

And they must stay the course. The vast majority of any organization's problems are problems with the system, with the way it does business. Since leaders control the system, they own the problems. As we've shown throughout this book, lean leaders solve those problems and seize new opportunities by putting the transformational management system in place—and keeping it there.

They are dogs on the bone of world-class performance.

CHAPTER TEN

Raising the Bar

In the 1950s, management guru Peter Drucker took issue with the scientific management model and its view of employees. He believed employees should be treated as assets, not liabilities, who work in "human communities" that promote trust and respect, and not just profits.

It was a hard sell. Most leaders had grown up with the scientific management model. They thought of their employees as cogs in a wheel, replaceable drones charged with repetitive tasks requiring little thought or initiative. When employees failed to do their simple jobs well, they were liabilities. When they joined their union friends on strike, they could not be trusted. The logical approach to managing them was a command-and-control hierarchy that ran every decision through the management structure.

We began this book by describing the limitations of this approach. Drucker saw those limitations fifty years ago, but they have been increasingly magnified by a growing global marketplace. When people become commodities and not a *human* resource, when they have no value beyond the tasks they perform, when they become expendable to boost the bottom line, we betray our very humanity. We give ourselves permission to exploit and repress others and, ultimately, to wage war without worrying about the casualties of war.

The new management model is one antidote to this destructive world view. While some may hold politicians accountable for world peace, we believe that all of us are accountable, and that we start with our communities—and that includes the "human communities" that we lead and in which we work. Rinaldo Brutoco, founder and president of the World Business Academy, put it this way:

> "While nations may not be ready to turn swords into ploughshares or to redesign the world economic order, the only way to ensure long-term sustainability and global security is to inspire investment in a world where the vision of peace, mutual benefit, and rising economic wealth for all supersedes the reality of a world crippled by fear, runaway military budgets, starvation, and saber-rattling." (from *What Is True Wealth & How Do We Create It*, by Verna Allee and Dinesh Chandra, Indigo Press, New Delhi, 2004)

Creating such a world requires new leaders who think big, who bring joy to the workplace, and who value the people who work with them to move their organization forward. Amazingly, this new brand of leadership also supports the growth and financial success companies seek. As we've noted throughout this book, competing globally requires speed and efficiency, and the new management model delivers them by making every employee an agent for change and continuous improvement.

So here we have the best of both worlds. We can create global "human communities" that promote trust and respect and, in the process, show people how they can coexist despite cultural, social, economic, and religious differences, while at the same time we are building transnational companies that meet financial goals by serving vast global markets.

For a long time, American businesses have been insulated from the rest of the world. We could grow comfortably—and often rapidly—by serving the diverse needs of a large population without ever having to look outside the U.S. The world came to us.

Such isolation is a luxury of the past. Today, most American companies are growing at an anemic 2 to 4 percent, if they're growing at all. Today, the greatest opportunities for growth lie outside the U.S., in China and India and Mexico and Brazil, and wherever else material wealth is beginning to escape the coffers of the powerful few. Local companies will seize these opportunities. They will design products their customers can afford and they will grow their market share, and then they will look to expand into the U.S. It's already happening.

JAIPUR FOOT

Here's one example. In India, it is estimated that nearly 10 million people suffer from locomotor disabilities, primarily caused by landmines. Landmines cover thousands of acres of Indian farmland along India's border with Pakistan. In the late 1960s, two doctors at the SMS Medical College in Jaipur, India, developed the Jaipur Foot as a low-cost alternative to the SACH prosthetic foot that costs $2,500 to $8,000 in the United States.

The Jaipur artificial limb has two parts, the foot piece and the socket with or without a joint, depending on whether the limb is needed above or below the knee. The initial design replaced heavy wooden sockets with lightweight, hand-crafted aluminum ones, which have since been replaced by high-density polyethylene that permits very rapid and accurate fitting.

Designing the foot for Indian customers posed unique problems, because they often squat rather than stand during conversations, and many do not wear shoes. Through the use of vulcanized rubber, the Jaipur Foot looks like a normal foot and allows squatting—two attributes the SACH foot does not provide. The company that makes the foot, Bhagwan Mahaveer Viklang Sahayata Samiti (BMVSS), is now working with the Indian Space Research Organisation, which is the Indian equivalent of NASA, to develop a polyurethane foot.

Since its inception in 1976, BMVSS has helped almost 780,000 disabled individuals walk through use of the Jaipur Foot and other ambulatory aids. This is what *Time* magazine wrote in 1997:

> "The beauty of the Jaipur Foot is its lightness and mobility—those who wear it can run, climb trees, and pedal bicycles—and its low price. While a prosthesis for a similar level of amputation can cost several thousand dollars in the U.S., the Jaipur Foot costs only $30 in India."

Donations cover the $30 cost, allowing BMVSS to fit nearly 780,000 people with prostheses so far, *free of charge*. Anyone can go to one of BMVSS's ten centers at any time without an appointment and will receive free room and board until they're ready to leave, which is typically the day after admission for below-knee amputees, and three days for above-knee amputees. The same process with the SACH foot can take three months. You can find out more about Jaipur Foot at www.jaipurfoot.org.

As BMVSS demonstrates, you cannot assume that all innovation will come from developed countries. The insularity of American companies has relegated too much of their research and development efforts to minor improvements on existing products and services. Their customers haven't changed. Their competitors haven't changed. Their capabilities haven't changed. As a result, their ability to generate breakthrough solutions—like their ability to grow—has become stagnant.

Exposure to customers outside the U.S. energizes a company by challenging it to serve different markets with different price points. Smaller companies often balk at going global because they aren't sure what to do, but there's a lot of help available. In any country where you want to do business, companies exist to help you understand and deal with the bureaucracy and legal system. TBM is a small company, but we haven't had any problem establishing offices overseas: We recently spent two weeks in China to set up an office there, and the process is becoming easier in India.

It's no longer enough just to export to other countries. Five years ago, that may have been sufficient, but now we must learn what customers in other countries require, understand their cultures, and customize our products and services to fit their unique needs. Toyota could have continued to build cars in Japan and export them to the U.S., but it understood that it needed a presence on American soil to grow market share. It put manufacturing and design facilities in the United States out of necessity to better understand and service American consumers.

Going global is also about more than outsourcing to get cheaper labor and raw materials. We invite every company that wants to outsource to China or India or Eastern Europe to also sell to those markets. It involves setting up operations in foreign countries, establishing joint ventures with foreign companies, listening to and learning from foreign customers, and getting entrenched in foreign markets. In the process, what is foreign becomes native. And your company has a global reach.

We've said this before, but it bears repeating: As markets grow, local companies develop products to serve them, and as these companies grow, as their expertise improves, they eventually turn their attention to U.S. markets and become your competitors here. Right now, you can choose to compete where the growing markets are. Wait, and the competition will come to you. Either way, the days of serving isolated markets are rapidly ending.

UNTENABLE APPROACHES TO MANAGEMENT

Anand has traveled extensively around the globe in the last thirty years and has seen many of the best and worst practices business can offer. He recently visited several small and medium-sized Indian manufacturing companies, all well-respected with excellent prospects for growth, and all with an alarming twist: They employ 20 to 80 percent of their workforce through intermediary contract labor providers. By agreement, these workers must be terminated in less than six months, which means every one of these companies has at least 100 percent turnover. When Anand asked about this strange behavior, the leaders said it had nothing to do with labor costs because there's an abundance of cheap labor available. In fact, in some cases they were paying more for the contract labor. Instead, management works with the labor providers to keep unions out, and to stay flexible enough to move to areas that offer incentives for their relocation.

It's a perfect example of treating people as disposable commodities, and it's not without its cost. It requires a large number of management people, many more than the amount needed by Western companies, to supervise the transient workforce. Since managers command higher salaries, huge management teams cost these companies a lot of money. Yet, despite the armies of management and technical people, poor quality and inconsistency plague these companies. And ironically, their approach is feeding the growing movement to organize into labor unions.

In the booming coastal regions of China, people coming from the interior to find jobs are being exploited with low wages, long hours, and poor working conditions that are neither humane nor sustainable. They are paid from $1,000 to $1,500 a year in the coastal regions, which is still several times more than people could earn in the interior. They work twelve hours a day, six days a week, in poor working and living conditions. Turnover ranges from 40 to 60 percent. This is not the right way, morally or economically, to treat people who are our most valuable asset.

As companies in the West have learned, if you treat people this way, you create apathetic workers who provide poor products and services to your customers. They've learned the hard way that you cannot have enough managers or supervisors or quality control inspectors to ensure quality products. Anand visited one manufacturing line in China whose rate of defective products was 35 percent, despite all the inspectors on the line. You have to get at the root cause of bad quality and remove it, and to do that you need well-trained, involved, and happy employees who care about the quality of their work.

The current movement in India and China is another mindless exercise to exploit people; it is the latest version of Taylor's scientific management system. And it's not limited to manufacturers. Anand visited a call center in India that hires bright recent graduates, "Americanizes" their names, and teaches them the pronunciation of approximately 500 English words so they can respond to their English-speaking callers. The novelty soon wears off for these bright young people, too many of whom turn to dangerous and destructive habits, such as smoking, drinking, and other forms of chemical dependencies, to bring some excitement into their lives. Turnover, which results from doing unsuitable and unchallenging work, can approach 100 percent per year. Ironically, the need for human resource professionals in India is growing 50 percent per year as companies hire more and more HR people to handle their high turnover rates.

If you look at Germany and France, you find the other extreme: Workers put in thirty-two to thirty-five hours a week and enjoy six weeks of vacation a year. Not only is this economically unfeasible, it results in high unemployment that leads to social unrest.

Neither extreme can survive the new market reality in which customers demand high-quality products and services at the right time and at the right price. Companies cannot meet these requirements unless they involve their employees in continually improving their processes. They may get by with treating employees like commodities for the short term, but as Western companies have painfully discovered, such an approach has a limited shelf life.

SOUND AND STRAIGHTFORWARD BUSINESS PRINCIPLES

Building a company with a social conscience is a once-in-a-lifetime opportunity for a visionary leader. In the first chapter, we described Henry Ford's innovative contributions to mass production, but Ford was also recognized for his attempts to treat his workers fairly. In 1914, he started paying workers five dollars for an eight-hour day, more than doubling wages for a shorter work day, paying semi-skilled workers more than other manufacturers were paying skilled craftsmen. Ford said, "There is one rule for the industrialist and that is: Make the best quality of goods possible at the lowest cost possible, paying the highest wages possible."

Of course, there is more to a quality work life than good wages. Indian industrialist Jamsetji Tata moved his steel company to an eight-hour day three years before Henry Ford. Tata believed that every company has a special responsibility to the communities where it is located and where its employees live. The company he created acts on that responsibility today by looking after 276 villages around the mines of Tata Steel. In 1895, Tata said, "We do not claim to be more unselfish, more generous, and more philanthropic than other people. But we think we started on sound and straightforward business principles, considering the interests of the shareholders our own, and the health and welfare of the employees [as] the sure foundation of our prosperity." Peter Drucker's belief in "human communities" may have been fifty years before its time, but Tata promoted the same concept sixty years before Drucker.

Treating people with respect, supporting their health and welfare, giving them challenging work, and providing opportunities for growth are "sound and straightforward business principles." We've experienced countless kaizen events and other improvement activities that involve employees in serving customers better, working more efficiently, and learning how to do a better job. We've found that value innovation is very egalitarian because it involves everyone in the company in serving customer needs— and it doesn't require a huge investment beyond reeducating employees to keep them relevant in an agile, customer-centric organization.

In Chapter 7, we described how companies use value innovation to become solutions providers to differentiate themselves, develop brand loyalty, lock in customers, and lead a very different race. Pursuing value innovation requires constantly reeducating people because listening to customers and meeting their changing needs means the products and services you offer will change, your processes will change, and the needs of people working those processes will change. You need to figure out how to help people remain relevant contributors to your success, and that makes constant reeducation both urgent and strategic.

When Art Learmonth was given the challenge of creating a service unit within Maytag, he found few people within the company who understood a service business. He had to develop people with that mindset, and that meant reeducation.

Companies also cannot ignore the more targeted education that will give them a technological edge. We've already lost that lead in this country by focusing more on people who can manage things and less on inventors and scientists. Technological innovation is based on basic research and requires people with scientific degrees whose job it is to reinvent the future.

Another area of education we need to target is a global perspective, the ability to navigate in different cultures, interact with and manage diverse groups of people, and communicate. We see a tremendous difference in cultural aptitude when we deal with people from Sweden, for example, than when we work with Americans, British, Germans, or French. The Swedes haven't had the luxury of operating solely within their borders, and they are better global competitors because of it.

Whether the need is for training in lean practices, reeducating workers, developing inventors and scientists, or creating cultural analysts, the goal is to become a learning organization. The key to becoming a learning organization is to invest in education and training. Too many companies look at the cost of training as an expense, rather than as an investment in the resource that is critical to their survival. When companies buy equipment, they set a budget for maintenance, and the same concept should hold for maintaining the knowledge and skills of your employees. At TBM, we spend in excess of $80,000 on each new consultant who joins us *before* they do any consulting. They go through twelve to sixteen weeks of "boot camp" training to understand the techniques and philosophy of our customer-focused approach. We've determined that's the minimum acceptable level to prepare them to be productive right from the start. We then involve them in two to four weeks of training per year to keep them prepared and help them remain relevant to our customers.

In a global marketplace, technological innovation is going to happen somewhere, in some part of the world, in every industry. Even if your company has the scientific and inventive capabilities to generate breakthrough discoveries, you have no control over how others will reinvent the future. But you do have control over the value innovation side of the equation. You control the processes that listen and respond to the Voice of the Customer. You control your ability to design, produce, and deliver the right products and services better and faster than the competition. And you control the contribution employees will make by training and reeducating them, trusting them, treating them with respect, and involving them in identifying and implementing the innovative practices that will help make your company a global leader.

LEVERAGING THE WORLD

Earlier this year, C.K. Prahalad, a noted author and professor at the University of Michigan Ross School of Business, delivered the keynote address at the 2005 SABA (South Asian Business Association) Conference at UCLA. He challenged the audience to recognize the market opportunity in serving five billion people in developing countries, which is 80 percent of the world's population. "How do you serve a consumer market when all you can see is abject poverty?" he asked. "Seeing a market at the bottom of the pyramid requires imagination, rather than analytics." Prahalad pointed out that serving this market challenges the assumptions we've made about serving the world's richest societies. Entrepreneurs and researchers, he said, must learn to marry low cost, good quality, sustainability, and profitability at the same time. If we can do that, Prahalad predicted the result could be a market as transformative as the Internet.

Prahalad gave three examples of the opportunities in developing countries, each of which relates to companies and industries we have discussed in this book.

He noted that while Indians travel—"It's like all of Scandinavia, and then some, on the move every day," he said—India's hospitality industry is largely undeveloped. To meet this market need, India's largest hotel chain created indiOne Hotels, opening the first hotel in Bangalore, with ten more scheduled to open by the end of 2006. Each indiOne Hotel offers clean rooms with LCD TVs, business centers, exercise equipment, and pleasant surroundings for about $20 a night. The first indiOne Hotel was profitable within a month. Prahalad calls it a model for global expansion.

Most new cars in India cost from four to five thousand dollars, and demand is growing. India's manufacturers have learned how to make high-quality automobile components for a fraction of what they cost in the U.S. The three areas in India where automobiles are made are the same areas where India's technology development is taking place. Prahalad suggested that India could revolutionize the automotive industry by combining automotive knowledge, manufacturing quality, small batch capability, low cost, and embedded software. Imagine the impact of a new $3,000 car on American markets.

The third example Prahalad presented was Jaipur Foot and the extraordinary innovation brought to serving the bottom of the pyramid. "I want you to think about innovative, high-tech solutions at new price and performance levels," he said. "Not five percent less, but five percent of what it costs here. This is the sandbox that the bottom of the pyramid forces you to play in ... But you can't do this unless you have imagination, passion, courage, a deep sense of humanity, and humility. We can do well and do good at the same time."

To be global leaders, we must draw upon the imagination and passion of our people to develop low-cost, high-quality products and services that serve all markets around the world. While a global leader does business worldwide, it doesn't necessarily do the same business worldwide. In the first chapter, we talked about deploying a global triad strategy to establish your "global footprint." The strategy addresses the different social and economic conditions in countries in what we call Zones 1, 2, and 3, which include: (1) China and India, where labor is cheap and consumer buying power is just beginning to grow; (2) Mexico, Brazil, and Eastern Europe, where costs are lower, but proximity to major markets is better; and, (3) United States, Europe, and Japan, where buying power is greatest and wages are highest.

A global leader creates centers of excellence in each of these zones and in all major parts of the world. For example, knowledge centers in

China and India can be combined with local manufacturing capabilities to supply standard products—nuts, bolts, baskets, etc., that have highly stable designs—at a low price point to internal or external customers in other parts of the world, as India has done with automotive components. More customized products, such as motors and control panels, can be produced in Mexico or Eastern Europe, also for delivery to internal or external customers. The final, customized solution can be developed in the U.S. or Europe, close to the customers, using parts and products made in the other two zones.

The final products and services can range from basic value offerings to high-end, vanity ones, with the best mix determined by customer needs in each market. For example, right now there is pent-up demand in China for high-end products from Europe and the U.S. A segment of consumers isn't interested in cheap imitations or alternatives, although other consumer segments in China are. A global company is positioned to provide

Figure 10-1   Model of a Global Business

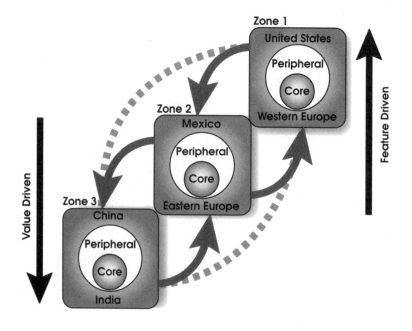

the right mix to meet the needs of all major segments, as shown in Figure 10-1.

In a truly global company, strategic direction, purpose and values, management development, brand equity, and access to capital markets are all global functions. Everything else is local. We propose five guiding principles for such a company:

1. Guarantee customer satisfaction unconditionally.
2. Pursue customer intimacy to understand stated and unarticulated needs.
3. Treat employees with respect and give them opportunities to grow and a real sense of ownership.
4. Create an environment where work is joyful and helps meet employees' material, social, and spiritual needs.
5. Give back to society by focusing on global issues that improve the quality of life for everyone.

One of these global issues is higher education. For some reason, parents get involved in the primary and secondary education of their children, but when the children go to college—and some of their parents become executives—parent involvement ends. As business leaders, they help direct funding to colleges and universities without expressing any interest in how that money is spent. It's our responsibility to make sure higher education balances the needs of society, students, and business to offer the practical knowledge that future employers will need. That means getting involved in shaping a better curriculum.

Education at all levels needs to focus on what's really needed, on practical and relevant knowledge, and not just on formulas and theories. If it does not, our ability to compete in a global marketplace, as companies and individuals, will be weakened. Our responsibility as business leaders is to awaken our education leaders to the new realities of global competition and to the promise it holds for a better world.

In India, states can decide on their own form of government. Two of the country's twenty-eight states democratically elected Marxist governments. One of these communist states, Kerala, chose to focus on education with amazing results: According to the 2001 census, its literacy rate was 91 percent, compared to less than 50 percent in the rest of India. That rate is even more impressive when you consider that Kerala educates nearly five million students. When you get off an airplane in Kerala, you quickly notice that something is different. Even if people are poor, they display the dignity that acquiring knowledge provides. As the state's General Education Department proudly notes, "The state has achieved a human development index comparable to the developed countries of the world." The department emphasizes that "the society attaches so much importance to education that the school in Kerala is really the nucleus of the social microcosm. Better education kindles the aspirations of the people..."

We couldn't agree more.

IN PURSUIT OF TRUE WEALTH

A friend of Anand's, Arun Wakhlu, is the founder, Chairman and Managing Director of Pragati Leadership Institute, a spiritually inspired development and consulting company specializing in Wholesome Leadership Development. It is based in Pune, India. Arun has designed and facilitated many new leadership development programs and has facilitated the development of more than 12,000 leaders. Fluent in five languages, Arun devotes a quarter of his time to socially relevant projects. His award winning book, *Managing from the Heart*, published in 1999 by Response Books (a division of Sage Publications), describes his vision of a future we are working for:

"Imagine a world where all people are at peace with themselves, and with each other, and living in an environment that is pure and green. Imagine a world where organizations exist for the total development of their own members. Where inspired working contributes to the well-being of planet Earth and its inhabitants. People working in such organizations would:
- Work with an abundance of energy and enthusiasm.

- Find work easy and fun.
- Make work so deeply joyful and rewarding that it would feel more like play rather than 'work.'

Such inspired work, done with joy in the heart, would be deeply liberating. It would be the creative engine for progress which, in turn, would unfold more joy. This freedom, progress, and joy is what the people of the world are thirsting for."

In our work helping organizations integrate the new management model, we often witness this thirst in the ways people react to the new challenges and opportunities it presents. The desires to do a better job, to feel enthusiastic about their work, and to enjoy what they do exist in all people, yet too few of us ever have the chance to act on those desires. Given the chance, most of us would choose to quench that thirst.

At the beginning of this book, we introduced Steve and Barb King and their company, Landscape Structures. The Kings have seen first-hand the human potential unleashed by moving to the new management model. "Kaizen teams have revealed new leaders among our employees," said Barb. "Talent is bubbling up in areas we never expected. And for all our concerns about lean, process-driven methods stifling our creativity, we have found the opposite has happened: Lean has actually enhanced our inventive impulses."

New leaders are waiting to surface in your organization. Talent is struggling for air. Inventive impulses await your command. We believe it is a leader's responsibility to release this energy, to sate this thirst, to create "human communities" that promote trust and respect and challenge people to achieve great things and to honor their achievements. In return, such leaders enjoy a true wealth that money cannot buy.

In *What Is True Wealth & How Do We Create It*, edited by Verna Allee and Dinesh Chandra and published by Indigo Press in 2004, Nigerian-born neurosurgeon Emeka Nchekwube offered his definition. Mr. Nchekwube, who currently lives and practices in San Jose, California, co-founded a company dedicated to developing affordable drugs for third-world markets. He wrote:

"True wealth, properly understood, is best appreciated in retrospect. Just as the true measure of a great tree can be taken only from what it leaves behind, so it is with the true wealth of a person. Did that person spawn new vibrant growth that could stand tall and confidently far into the future? Create a tide that lifted all boats? Leave light where there was darkness, love where there was hate, food where there was hunger? And did that person leave behind someone inspired to continue his quest?"

When you think about great American companies, you think of the visionary leaders who found innovative ways to solve common problems. Although a global marketplace exposes new problems, we are already seeing the next generation of visionary leaders hard at work solving them.

In this book, we have offered you a look at our antidote to the poison of old-style, command-and-control management, whose time has clearly come and gone. With more and more companies facing stiff global competition, now is the time for a new system that goes beyond the top-down approach of years' past and addresses the extreme challenges of the twenty-first century. Through our transformational management system, we provide an innovative way forward, a path that will help you define your own journey and set your organization apart from a growing field of global competitors.

We challenge your company to step onto the global stage by getting your house in order through operational excellence, aligning supply and demand to synchronize with the Voice of the Customer, and pursuing value innovation to grow as a solutions provider. The journey will renew your passion for the work to be done. It will engage employees in learning and contributing. It will strengthen your company, your communities, your industry, your country, and your world. It will allow you to do well and do good at the same time.

And it will generate true wealth that inspires, enlightens, and elevates us all.

APPENDIX

Overcoming Obstacles

In our experiences helping hundreds of organizations integrate the transformational management system, we encounter the same barriers over and over again. It doesn't matter what size the organization is or what it does, the same obstacles impede their journeys. We propose the following countermeasures to ensure that the antidote works.

	Barrier	Problem	Countermeasures
1	Change in leadership	New leaders do not share their predecessors' commitment.	• If possible, "screen for lean" to hire leaders who believe in the transformational management system.
			• Educate new leaders on your journey and the measurable benefits already achieved.
2	Leaders not on board	Some existing leaders resist the transformation.	• Apply the principles in your department and unit and build on your results.
			• Create too much momentum for the resisters to stop it.
			• Produce "extreme" results and give the resister credit for it.
			• Replace resisters with believers.

Barrier	Problem	Countermeasures
3 Inside-out thinking	Unrealistic view of own and competitors' capabilities.	• Bring reality into the organization through customer forums, competitive analysis, SWOT analysis. • Involve more employees in Voice of the Customer activities. • Identify sources of "outside in" information and widely communicate that information.
4 Short-term focus	Settle for short-term gains.	• Teach and communicate often that this is a journey. • Communicate that the transformation is not only about cutting costs: It is about growth. • Link short-term gains to long-term goals
5 "Hockey-stick" mentality	Focus on end of the week/ month/ quarter/year; promotes firefighting and "heroes" who save the day.	• Focus on creating flow, getting in a rhythm that evens out demand and supply—and results. • Recognize the new "heroes" who do their jobs well and efficiently every day. • Build a culture of continuous improvement to replace a culture of firefighting.
6 Financially driven culture	Exclusive focus on getting quarterly/annual financial results.	• Involve employees in those activities that are critical to continuous improvement and growth, such as improving quality, solving problems, and participating in Voice of the Customer activities. • Recognize and reward performance on more than just financial results.
7 Lack of trust	People believe management will use cost-cutting to lay people off.	• Be firm, fair, consistent, and equitable. • Help employees understand the benefits—to them and the organization—of what you are asking them to do.

Barrier	Problem	Countermeasures
8 Lack of accountability	Results not achieved because people aren't held accountable for them.	• Set clear, measurable goals for people. • Review performance on these goals at regular intervals. • Hold people accountable for this performance—and provide assistance as needed.
9 Lack of discipline	People "lay low" and wait for the energy to dissipate.	• Follow the same review process every time, month after month, quarter after quarter, year after year, until a new discipline is embedded.
10 Business process resistance	Those not in production or operations fear the loss of their power base.	• Make the case for involving everyone in the transformation. • Emphasize that flexibility is critical. • Reassure people that the source of power now resides in their ability to work efficiently across functions to achieve the company's goals and objectives.
11 Regression	Journey stalls as people revert to old habits.	• Teach leaders, managers, supervisors, and employees how to build a countermeasure culture. • Be prepared to try "Plan B" to sustain the transformation, which means having several Plan Bs ready to go.

About the Authors

ANAND SHARMA

Recognized as "A Hero of US Manufacturing" by *Fortune* magazine, Anand has worked beside the Japanese pioneers who founded the famed Toyota Production System (TPS). In 2002, he received the Donald Burnham Manufacturing Management Award from the Society of Manufacturing Engineers. A leading consultant and strategist to CEOs of Fortune 1000 companies on five continents, he has personally led productivity improvements, innovation, and growth at hundreds of enterprises that have emerged as market leaders.

Anand is the president and CEO of TBM Consulting Group, Inc., which has grown over the past 15 years to be the worldwide leader in "lean innovation" and business improvement. With more than 20 years of line management experience within the manufacturing industry, he is a frequent lecturer on global manufacturing and enterprise performance.

He is also the author of *The Perfect Engine: How to Win in the New Demand Economy by Building to Order with Fewer Resources* (Free Press, 2001) and holds a Masters Degree in Business Administration from

Boston University and undergraduate degree in Mechanical Engineering from Roorkee University in India.

GARY HOURSELT

As executive vice president of International Consulting and Strategy at TBM Consulting Group, Inc., and a former senior executive in the aerospace industry, Gary provides broad expertise in lean business strategy development and deployment to TBM's Strategy Practice. Gary has helped many of TBM's client companies leverage their LeanSigma® gains to achieve significant growth. In addition to his expertise in LeanSigma transformation, he is an authority on industrial strategy, growth leadership, and execution.

During his five years as president of Huck Fastening Systems' industrial and aerospace divisions, revenues nearly doubled, pre-tax income increased over 700 percent, and return on investment nearly quadrupled. He has also led the acquisition and integration of four global businesses in four years.

A Certified Public Accountant, Gary has led companies throughout Canada, China, France, Germany, Great Britain, India, Italy, Japan Mexico, and the United States. He has an MBA from Northern Illinois University and a Bachelor's degree from Aurora University.

Anand and Gary may be contacted at the following address:
TBM Consulting Group, Inc.
4400 Ben Franklin Blvd.
Durham, NC 27704
800-438-5535
http://www.tbmcg.com